NORTH CAROLINA SLAVES
AND
FREE PERSONS OF COLOR

IREDELL COUNTY

William L. Byrd, III
and John H. Smith

HERITAGE BOOKS
2007

HERITAGE BOOKS
AN IMPRINT OF HERITAGE BOOKS, INC.

Books, CDs, and more—Worldwide

For our listing of thousands of titles see our website
at
www.HeritageBooks.com

Published 2007 by
HERITAGE BOOKS, INC.
Publishing Division
65 East Main Street
Westminster, Maryland 21157-5026

Copyright © 2002 William L. Byrd, III
and John H. Smith

All rights reserved. No part of this book may be reproduced or transmitted in any form or by any means, electronic or mechanical, including photocopying, recording or by any information storage and retrieval system without written permission from the author, except for the inclusion of brief quotations in a review.

International Standard Book Number: 978-0-7884-2088-7

"As I crawled between decks, I could not imagine how this little army was to be packed or draw breath in a hold but twenty-two inches high!... we made them lie down in each other's laps, like sardines in a can, and in this way obtained space for the entire cargo."
--Capt. Theodore Canot, *Adventures of an African Slaver* (1854)[1]

---

[1] James Nichols, *The Life of Olaudah Equiano, or Gustavus Vassa, the African* (1814; reprint, New York: Dover Publications, 1999) iii

Contents

Introduction — *vii*

Acknowledgements — *ix*

Chapter One — *1*
  Iredell County — 1
    Criminal Actions — 1

Chapter Two — *79*
  Iredell County — 79
    Civil Actions — 79

Chapter Three — *169*
  Iredell County — 169
    Miscellaneous Records — 169

Chapter Four — *173*
  Iredell County — 173
    Petitions to Sell Slaves — 173

Appendix A — *177*
  Glossary of Legal Terms — *177*

Table of Cases — *179*
  Civil and Criminal Actions — 179

Index — *183*

Introduction

The records in this book were transcribed from original papers located in the North Carolina State Archives. Most of these papers are listed under general headings such as "Slaves and Free Negroes, " or "Slaves and Free Persons of Color." Occasionally they are listed under the heading of "Miscellaneous Records."[2]

This particular group of papers were selected from the North Carolina county of Iredell. Not a few of these records are torn and faded. In some cases, part of the original text is missing, and many of the names of individuals are almost indecipherable. Nevertheless, every attempt has been made to transcribe these papers as accurately as possible.

Included are a plethora of civil and criminal actions pertaining to slaves and free persons of color. The interactions between both Blacks and Whites are displayed on an antagonistic and intimate level, and are dramatically played out through crime and punishment. The criminal cases are filled with intrigue involving murder, felonies, trading with slaves and harboring slaves.

---

[2] Thornton W. Mitchell, "Preliminary Guide to Records Relating to Blacks in the North Carolina State Archives," *Archives Information Circular* 17(June 1980): 3-4.

The different sections of this book are broken down into the following categories: Civil Actions, Criminal Actions, Miscellaneous Records, and Petitions to Sell Slaves.

Iredell County was established in 1789, and was named in honor of James Iredell of Edenton. Iredell County is located in the central section of the State, and is bounded by Rowan, Cabarrus, Mecklenburg, Lincoln, Catawba, Alexander, Wilkes, Yadkin, and Davie counties. A portion of Burke and Wilkes was annexed to Iredell in 1793, and part of Iredell was annexed to Wilkes in 1815. In 1818, portions of Wilkes and Burke were added to Iredell[3]

---

[3] David Leroy Corbitt, *The Formation of the North Carolina Counties: 1663-1943* (Raleigh: Division of Archives and History, 1950) 127-128

Acknowledgements

All acknowledgements regarding this book belong to the staff of the North Carolina State Archives. Without their help, it would not have been possible.

Iredell County
Criminal Actions

Chapter One

Iredell County

Criminal Actions

North Carolina State Archives
Iredell County Records
Records of Slaves and Free Persons of Color
C.R.054.928.2

State Vs. Tom, (a Slave)
Criminal Actions
Attempted Rape
Iredell County, NC [1853]

State of North Carolina   }
Mecklenburg County   }

     Whereas information hath been [?] to me F.M. Ross one of the acting Justices of the peace for the County aforesaid on the oath of Mary A. Gribble that Tom a slave the property of Robert F. Davidson of the County aforesaid did on the 10th day of September A.D. 1853 [?] the body of Mary A. Gribble of the said County at and in the County aforesaid then and there in the peace of God and the State.

Iredell County
Criminal Actions

[Assault with intent to rape & ravish the said Mary Gribble against the peace and dignity of the State.]

This is therefore to command you to arrest the body of the said Tom (a slave) and have him before some Justice of the Peace of said County to answer to said complaint and be further dealt with according to law - Herein fail not & have you then and there this Warrant.

Given under my hand & seal this 12th day of September A.D.

F.M. Ross   (Seal)
Executed, T.N. Alexander

State Vs Tom (a slave)

The defendant Tom being brought before me F.M. Ross one of the Justices of said County and charged according to the [?] of the foregoing Warrant and being put on his examination says that he is not guilty of the assault with intent to rape as charged in said Warrant.

Mary Gribble, Witness for this State being duly sworn states

That she was on the way home from town between five and six oclock on the afternoon of Saturday the tenth on horseback just as I got to the corner of Betsy [?] old field my horse freightened, I [?] to the mare when someone said yes - I looked up and saw a negro boy - dressed in a clean looking shirt and briches - bare headed - he asked me if I was Miss Gribble - I told him yes - he then asked me how far it was to our house - I told him it was but a little bit - then he caught hold of the beast by the bridle - I screamed & called Billy - he then held the bridle with his left hand & caught hold of me with the other - I struck him three or four times with my fist but the saddle turned and I fell off - we scuffled a good while in the road - I still screamed - he caught me by the [?] [?] he threw me down so that I fell on the right hand side of the road on my [?] - I jumped up and he then run - he tried to throw me down all the time when scuffling - I thought at this time and still think that his intention was to commit a rape on me.

The Defendant - the property of Robert F. Davidson - is the identical boy who committed the assault on me.

The assault was committed in this County about one mile and a half from town - between five and six oclock on last Saturday evening September 1853
F.M. Ross

Iredell County
Criminal Actions

On the foregoing examination it is hereby ordered and adjudged that Tom the defendant, be committed to the jail of said County, & the Sheriff of the County is hereby commanded to keep said Boy Tom in the Walls of said jail, & not to receive bond for his appearance until he is further dealt with according to Law at our next Sup. Court
Sep 12 1853
F.M. Ross, JP   (Seal)

State Vs. Tom, (a slave)
Special Venire
Executed, H Troutman, Shff
1853

State of North Carolina
To the sheriff of Iredell County greetings
You are hereby commanded to summon fifty Jurors, freeholders and slave holders, (a special Venire) to be and appear at the Court House in Statesville on Tuesday of this Term at half past 9 O'clock A.M.
Spring Term 1853
C.L. Summers, Clk

State Vs. Tom, (a slave)
Subp. For the State
To Spring Term 1854, Iredell
Executed by T N Alexander, Shff
To hand 31st March
S.N. Hutchinson, Wit.

State of North Carolina

To the Sheriff of Mecklenburg County - Greeting, You are hereby commanded to summon S.N. Hutchinson personally to be and appear before the Judge of our Superior Court of Law, at the next Court to be held for Iredell County, at the Court-House in Statesville on the 1st Monday after the 4th Monday in March next, then and there to testify and the truth to say, in behalf of the State in a certain matter of controversy before said Court depending, and then and there to be tried, wherein the State is

Iredell County
Criminal Actions

plaintiff, and (Tom a slave) is defendant. And this you shall in no wise omit, under the penalty prescribed by law.

Witness, JB Kerr Clerk of our said Court at office the 7th Monday after the 4th Monday in September and in the seventy-7th Year of our Independence, Anno Domini 1853.
JB Kerr, Clk SC

Subp. 1853
The State Vs. Tom (a slave)
Executed, TN Alexander, Shff
To hand 31st March 1854

State of North Carolina

To the Sheriff of Mecklenburg County - Greeting:
You are hereby commanded to summon George Plummer personally to be and appear before the Judge of our Superior Court of Law, at the next Court to be held for our said County, at the Court-House in Statesville on the 1st Monday after the 4th Monday in March next; then and there to testify, and the truth to say in behalf of Tom (a slave) in a certain matter of controversy before said Court depending, and then and there to be tried, wherein the State is Plaintiff and Tom is Defendant. And this you shall in no wise omit, under the penalty prescribed by Law.

Witness, CL Summers, Clerk of our said Court at Office, the 1st Monday after the 4th Monday in September 1853 and in the 77th Year of our Independence.
C.S. Summers, Clk
By C.A. Carlton, D Clk

Subpoena, 1853
State Vs. Tom (a slave)
Subpoena for F.W. Ross for Deft.
Executed, T.N. Alexander, Shff
To hand 28th March 1854

State of North Carolina
To the Sheriff of Mecklenburg County - Greeting:

Iredell County
Criminal Actions

You are hereby commanded to summon Francis W. Ross personally to be and appear before the Judge of our Superior Court of Law, at the next Court to be held for our said County, at the Court-House in Statesville on the 4th Monday after the 4th Monday in March next; then and there to testify, and the truth to say in behalf of Tom (a slave) in a certain matter of controversy before said Court depending, and then and there to be tried, wherein the State is Plaintiff and the said Tom is Defendant. And this you shall in no wise omit, under the penalty prescribed by law.

Witness, C.L. Summers Clerk of our said Court at Office, the 1st Monday after the 4th Monday in September 1853 and in the 76th year of our Independence
C.L. Summers, Clk
By C.A. Carlton, D Clk

Subpoena, 1853
State Vs. Tom (a slave)
Subpoena for S.A. Harris, P. Torrence & R.W. White, for Deft.
Executed on Harris & Torrence only White not to be found in my County
He has gone to South Carolina
T.N. Alexander, Shff
To hand 28th March 1854

State of North Carolina
To the Sheriff of Mecklenburg County - Greeting:

You are hereby commanded to Summon Samuel A. Harris, Oni Torrence & Robert White personally to be and appear before the Judge of our Superior Court of Law, at the next Court to be held for our said County, at the Court-House in Statesville on the 1st Monday after the 4th Monday in March next; then and there to testify, and the truth to say in behalf of Tom, a slave, in a certain matter of controversy before said Court depending, and then and there to be tried, wherein the State is Plaintiff and the said Tom is Defendant.

And this you shall in no wise omit, under the penalty prescribed by Law. Witness, C.S. Summers Clerk of our said Court at Office, the 1st Monday after the 4th Monday in September 1853 and in the 77th Year of our Independence.
C.S. Summers, Clk
By C.A. Carlton, D Clk

Iredell County
Criminal Actions

State Vs. Tom, a slave } Iredell Sup. Court
Property of Robert F. Davidson } Spring 1853

The Slave was arraigned & Tried upon the following indictment viz.

 There is no exception to the various rulings of the Court upon the trial, but after the verdict which is set forth in the record.
 The prisoner's counsel moved for arrest of judgment for various defects appearing upon the face of the record & in the bill of indictment.
 Viz The motion being over ruled & judgment of death pronounced upon the Prisoner. An appeal was prayed & granted.
 M.E. Manly, Judge

State   } Superior Court of law
Vs.   } Fall Term
Tom a Slave }

 R F Davidson the owner of the defendant in this case maketh oath that he is **[Blank]** and believes that much excitement and prejudice exist in the County of Mecklenburg against the defendant in this case that the subject of the prosecution has been much canvassed - and that such is the state of public sentiment that he does not believe he can have a fair trial in this County.

Sworn to in open Court, 15 Nov 1853
Robt. Davidson
J B Kerr, Clk

State Vs. Tom, a slave
Iredell Superior Court of Law
Spring Term 1854

 R.F. Davidson (Master of Tom) maketh oath that this case cannot be safely tried without the testimony of Samuel A Harris and Robert White. Said Harris resides in the town of Charlotte and is absent on account of sickness. Said witness is under subpoena and is absent without the consent or procurement of this office, had a Subpoena issued for

Iredell County
Criminal Actions

Robert White which is [?] not to be found, said witness is absent without his consent in [?] this applicant states that he expects to have the benefit of the testimony of both witnesses at the next term of this court and that this applicant is not made for delay.
R.F. Davidson
Sworn to before Mr. C.S. Summers, Clk

State Vs Tom, a slave
Iredell Superior Court of Law
Spring Term 1855

  R.F. Davidson - Master of Slave Tom maketh oath that this case cannot be safely tried at this term for the want of Samuel A Harris a witness who is under subpoena and absent from this Court on account of sickness, Defendant expects to prove by said witness that the tracks alleged to be defendant's did not correspond with the foot of defendant - as appeared leading across the field to where the assault is alleged to have been Committed - that applicant expects to have the benefit of said witnesses Testimony at the next term of this Court.
R.F. Davidson
Sworn to before me
C.S. Summers, Clk

Execution made - known to the Clerk
S.C. Mecklenburg County
17th July 1854
T.N. Alexander, Shff
To hand, 15th July 1854
T.N. Alexander, Shff

State of North Carolina
To the sheriff of Mecklenburg County Greetings:
  Whereas at spring term of our Superior Court of Law began & held for the County of Iredell at the Court House in Statesville on the 1st Monday after the 4th Monday in March 1854 A diminution of the Record was suggested in the Case The State Vs Tom (a Slave) from Mecklenburg. Whereupon it is ordered and adjudged by the Court that the Clerk of the Superior Court of the County of Mecklenburg bring up from said Court a

Iredell County
Criminal Actions

more perfect Transcript of the Record in this case. These are therefore to Command to you make the premises known to the said Clerk & That you summon him to bring up a record perfect Transcript of the Records in said Case to our next Superior Court to be held for the County of Iredell at the Court House in Statesville the 1st Monday after the 4th Monday in September next herein fail not and have then & there this writ, Witness C.S. Summers, Clerk of our said Court at Office the 1st Monday after the 4th Monday in March AD 1854
C.S. Summers, Clk

Transcript of Statement to Iredell with postage cost
Meck. Co. Bill of Costs

State Vs Tom (a Slave) - Rape
Transcript to Spring Term 1854
Iredell County, Postage 15 cts.

State of North Carolina } Superior Court
Mecklenburg County   } of Law

   Be it remembered that at a Superior Court of Law begun and held for the County of Mecklenburg aforesaid at the Court House in Charlotte on the 7th Monday after 4th Monday in September in the Year of our Lord one thousand Eight Hundred & fifty three before the Honorable John M. Dick, Judge, Thos. N. Alexander Sheriff of said County, makes return, that in obedience to the writ of Venire Facias, heretofore to him directed, he has Summoned the following Jurors to wit, Lorenzo Hunter, Wm Means, David W Barnet, Wm Gray, Alexander Cooper, Batte Irwin, JJ Berryhill, Chs T Alexander, Wm Browne, W.G. Philips, Chs T Means, Jas Wallace, Robert A. McNeely, John G. Maxwell, Wilson M. Miller, Wm Rea, F.H. Maxwell, David M. Henderson, William Stinson, Jas N. Ross, Thos Gibson, Samuel Flanniken, Jas B. Robinson, Robert Ormand, Robert H. Young, Wm. Hutchinson, George Campbell, E.C. Wallace, Wm Lee, A.R. Irwin, Jonathan Lewis, Tobias Wolf, George C. Cathey, John Kirk, Saml. B. Hall & Joseph N. Rhyne and thereupon by the Oath of Wm Rea, Jas. N. Ross, John G. Maxwell, E.C Wallace, David M. Henderson, George Campbell, David W Barnet, Samuel Flanniken, Jas. B. Robinson, Wm. Meanse, A.R. Erwin, Lorenzo Hunter, Wm. Lee, Joseph N Rhyne, Jonathan Lewis, Robert A. McNeely, Samuel B. Hall, & GC Cathey good

Iredell County
Criminal Actions

and lawful men of the County aforesaid then and there drawn from the said Venire and the and there Empannelled, Sworn, and Charged to inquire for the State of and Concerning all crimes and offences Committed within the Body of the said County; it is presented in manner and form following, that is to say:

State of North Carolina } Superior Court of Law
Mecklenburg County } Fall Term 1853

    The Jurors for the State upon their Oath present that Tom a person of Color and a Slave the property of Robert F. Davidson late of the County of Mecklenburg on the the tenth day of September in the year of our Lord one thousand Eight hundred & fifty three, with force and arms at and in the County of Mecklenburg aforesaid in and upon the body of Mary A. Gribble (a white female) in the Peace of God and the State then and there being, violently and feloniously did make an assault, and her the said Mary A Gribble then and there did beat, wound and ill treat with intention her the said Mary A Gribble violently and against her will then and there feloniously to ravish and Carnally Know and other wrongs to the said Mary A. Gribble Contrary to the form of the Statutes in Such Case made and provided and against the peace and dignity of the State.
Landers [Sanders], Sol.

[?] which Bill of Indictment is the following Endorsements to wit.
Wm Gribble, Mary A Gribble
Sworn & sent 14 Nov 1853
J.B. Kerr, Clk
"A True Bill" Wm Rea, Foreman.

And at the Term aforesaid (to wit Fall Term 1853) the following appears of record to wit.
    "Process waived and notice admitted by R.F. Davidson the Owner of the defendant, And the said Tom (a person of Color and a Slave the property of R.F. Davidson) is brought to the Bar of the Court & here in his proper person by the Said Thomas N Alexander, Sheriff of Mecklenburg County in whose Custody he is - And forth with it being demanded of him how he will acquit himself of the premises in the Indictment above specified and charged upon him he saith "He is not guilty thereof" And thereof for good and for Evil he puts himself upon the Country, And

Iredell County Criminal Actions

William Sanders Esqr Solicitor who prosecutes for the State on this behalf doth the like.

And at the Term aforesaid (to wit Fall Term 1853) the following order is made to wit, "Upon affidavit of R. F. Davidson the owner of the defendant it is ordered by the Court that this Case be removed to Iredell County for Trial"
Further it is ordered by the Court that the Sheriff of Mecklenburg County deliver the defendant Tom to the Sheriff of Iredell County on Wednesday after 4th Monday in March next.

The following is the Copy of the affidavit filed for removal to wit:

State Vs. Tom (a Slave) - Superior Court of Law Fall Term 1853
"R.F. Davidson the Owner of the defendant in this Case maketh oath that he is advised and believes that much excitement and prejudice Exist in the County of Mecklenburg against the defendant in this case that the subject of the prosecution has been much Canvassed and that such is the State of public sentiment that he does not believe he can have a fair Trial in this County."
Robt. F. Davidson
Sworn to in open Court 15 Nov 1853 - JB Kerr, Clk

State of North Carolina } Superior Court
Mecklenburg County } of Law

I Jennings B Kerr, Clk of the Superior Court of Law of said County do hereby Certify that the foregoing Contains a full true and perfect Transcript of the Case therein recited.

In Testimony whereof I have hereunto set my hand and affixed the seal of said Court at Office this 20th March 1854.
J.B. Kerr, CSC

Bill of costs - Mecklenburg County
Clk JB Kerr	3.80
TN Alexander, Shff	1.30
Wm Berryhill	.90
Thos S Boyd, DS	6.80
Wm Gribble, SW	1.38
Mary A Gribble	1.38

Iredell County
Criminal Actions

Thos S Boyd, SW   1.30

State of North Carolina   } Superior Court of Law
Mecklenburg County   } Fall Term 1853

State Vs. Tom, a Slave

Ordered by the Court that the Sheriff of Mecklenburg County deliver the defendant to the Sheriff of Iredell County on Wednesday after the fourth Monday in March next.
Test, J B Kerr, Clk SC

State Vs. Tom (a Slave)
Order of Court
Fall Term 1853

Executed by delivering the Prisoner Tom to the Shff of Iredell on Wednesday the 29th 1854.
T.N. Alexander, Shff of Mecklenburg Co.
To hand 28th March 1854

State Vs. Tom (a Slave)
Subp for the State - To Spring Term 1855

1st Monday after 4th Monday in March 1855 - To Statesville
Executed
E.C. Greer, Shff
J.P. Gillaspie, JP
Pinkney Berryhill

I E.C. Grier Shff Depute JP Gillaspie to Execute the within

State of North Carolina
To the Sheriff of Mecklenburg County Greeting
You are hereby commanded to Summon Pinckney Berryhill personally to be and appear before the Judge of our Superior Court of Law at the next Court to be held for Iredell County, at the Court-House in Statesville on the 1st Monday after the 4th Monday in March next, then and

Iredell County
Criminal Actions

there to testify, and the truth to say, in behalf of the State in a certain matter of controversy before said Court depending, and then and ther to be tried, wherein the State is Plaintiff, and Tom (a Slave the property of R.F. Davidson is defendant   And this you shall in no wise omit, under the penalty prescribed by law.

Witness, J.B. Kerr Clerk of our said Court, at Office the 1st Monday after the 4th Monday in September and in the seventy 9th year of our Independence A.D. 1854
J.B. Kerr, CM SC

Transporting Costs
E.C. Greer
Act for Bringing Tom from Charlotte to Statesville

40 Miles @ 10	4.00
" Miles @ 5	2.00
1 Days Board	.50
	6.50

Iredell County Court Costs
State Vs. Tom (a Slave)

Solicitor	10.00
Bill in Iredell Superior Court	
Docketing	1.00
3 Copt	.90
25 Seals	3.75
2 Affidavits	.40
4 Orders	.80
1 Rule & Motion	.30
Certiorari & Seal	1.25
Appeal Bond	.60
Judgment & Bill	1.10
5 Supp	.75
3 Seals	.75
Postage	[?]
1 Capias for Defts with Seal	1.00
Jury	.10

Iredell County
Criminal Actions

JB Kerr 2 Supps	3.75
2 Seals	6.25
Postage 6--	
Shff Ross for 75 Venire 20) 15./ 2 Subp	15.60
2/3 Subps TN Alexander	6.90
Shf $2 Suby 60) 50 Venire [?] 10.00	10.60
Delivering slave to Shff Charlotte	
R Watts Shff	.30
D.S. Smith	.30
D.S. Gillespie	.30
EC Greer Shff for delivering Slave	6.50
JD Cashion to the use of T Hall [?]	15.82
Nancy Jones " " " " W.S. Normant	15.82
J.K. Chatham to AC McIntosh see Reps file	10.69
R.R. Shaw	15.70
Oni Torrence to R Shaw	9.80
WP McLelland	15.70
G. [?] for State	15.70
" " for Defts	15.70
Silva Jones (a Slave)	15.70
Richard [?]	17.30
M. Hutchinson	15.82
One Torrence to Alonzo Walker	5.94
Wm Gribbles	11.53 1/3
Mary A Gribble	11.53 1/3
Worrey a slave of John Young	2.72
A.A. Kenneday	15.70
Jos. Meade	11.88
F.M. Ross for Deft	11.80
" " for State	11.80
TC Allison	15.70
MB Taylor	11.56
R.S. Reid	3.50

State of North Carolina
To the Sheriff of Mecklenburg County Greeting

     Whereas at Spring Term of our Superior Court of Law began & held for the County of Iredell at the Court House in Statesville on the 1st

Iredell County
Criminal Actions

Monday after the 4th Monday in March 1854 A diminution of the Record was suggested in the Case. The State Vs. Tom (a Slave) from Mecklenburg. Whereupon it is ordered and adjudged by the Court that the Clerk of the Superior Court of the County of Mecklenburg bring up from said Court a more perfect Transcript of the Record in this Case. These are therefore to Command to you make the premises known to the said Clerk & that you Summon him to bring up a more perfect Transcript of the Records in said Case to our next Superior Court to be held for the County of Iredell at the Court House in Statesville the 1st Monday after the 4th Monday in September next. Herein fail not and have you then & there this Writ, Witness C.S. Summers, Clerk of our said Court at Office the 1st Monday after the 4th Monday in March AD 1854.
C.S. Summers, Clk
To hand 15th July 1854, T.N. Alexander

Execution made known to the Clerk S.C.
Mecklenburg County 17th July 1854
T.N. Alexander, Shff

State Vs Tom, a Slave
Superior Court Decision
August Term 1855

State of North Carolina
Superior Court - at Morganton
August Term 1855

The State Vs Tom a person of Color } From Iredell
The property of Robert F Davidson } County

     This cause coming on to be argued upon the transcript of the record from the Superior Court of Law for the County of Iredell upon consideration thereof this Court is of opinion that there is no error in the proceedings of the said Superior Court of Law. Whereupon it is considered and adjudged by the Court here that this be certified to the said Superior Court of Law for the County of Iredell to the intent said Superior Court of Law proceed to Judgment and its execution according to law.

A True Copy

Iredell County
Criminal Actions

Test, Jas R Dodge, Clk

State Vs. Tom, a Slave
Writ - Vinire
Executed, J.A. Rosebro, Shff

State of North Carolina
To the sheriff of Iredell County

    Ordered by the Court that You Summon 15 freeholders & slave holders as a special vinire to appear on Wednesday morning Spring Term 1855.

State Vs Tom (a Slave)
Subp Inst - to Spring 1855
Executed, H. Troutman, Shff

State of North Carolina
    To the Sheriff of Iredell County- Greeting:
You are hereby commanded to Summon Robert S. Reid personally to be and appear before the Judge of our Superior Court of Law, at the next Court to be held for our said County, at the Court-House in Statesville on the 1st Monday after the 4th Monday in March (Inst) next; then and there to testify, and truth to say in behalf of the State in a certain matter of controversy before said Court depending, and then and there to be Tried, wherein the State is Plaintiff and Tom, a Slave of R.F. Davidson is Defendant. And this you shall in no wise omit, under the penalty prescribed by Law.
    Witness, C.S. Summers Clerk of our said Court at Office, the 1st Monday after the 4th Monday in March 1855 and in the year of our Independence.
C.S. Summers, Clk

Order of the Superior for removal of Tom

Executed by Delivering the Boy Tom to the Sheriff at Mecklenburg
H. Troutman, Shff

Iredell County
Criminal Actions

Executed by Delivering the Boy to the Jailor at Statesville
March 28th 1855
E.C. Greer, Shff

State of North Carolina   } Superior Court of Law
Iredell County   } Fall Term 1854

       Upon execution it is ordered by the Court that the Sheriff of the County of Iredell deliver the Prisoner Tom to the Sheriff of the County of Mecklenburg to be by him safely kept in the Jail of the said County & delivered to the Sheriff of the County of Iredell on or before the Monday of the next Superior Court of the said County of Iredell.
C.S. Summers, Clk

State Vs Tom (a Slave)
Subp (Inst) To Spring 1855
Executed, H. Troutman, Shff

State of North Carolina.
To the Sheriff of Iredell County-Greeting:
       You are hereby commanded to Summon Archibald Hill personally to be and appear before the Judge of our Superior Court of Law, at the next Court to be held for our said County, at the Court-House in Statesville on the 1st Monday after the 4th Monday in March (Inst) next; then and there to testify, and the truth to say in behalf of the State in a certain matter of controversy before said Court depending, and then and there to be Tried, wherein the State is Plaintiff and Tom (a Slave) of R.F. Davidson is Defendant. And this you shall in no wise omit, under the penalty prescribed by Law.
       Witness, C.S. Summers Clerk of our said Court at Office, the 1st Monday after the 4th Monday in March 1855 and in the **[Blank]** year of our Independence.
C.S. Summers, Clk

State Vs Tom (a Slave)
Transcript
Certioran [?]

Iredell County
Criminal Actions

Postage to Clk, Summers, 23 cts.

State of North Carolina   }
Mecklenburg County   }

    Be it known that at a Superior Court of Law began & held for the County of Mecklenburg aforesaid at the Court House in Charlotte on the 7th Monday after the 4th Monday in September one thousand Eight hundred & fifty three it being the 14th day of November in said year the honorable John M. Dick, Judge presiding, then Thomas N. Alexander high Sheriff of said County returned into Court a writ of Venire Facias in the following words and figures to wit.

" State of North Carolina
To the Sheriff of Mecklenburg County Greetings:
    You are hereby commanded to Summon the following named persons to be and appear at our next Superior Court of Law to be held for the County aforesaid at the Court House in Charlotte on the 7th Monday after the 4th Monday in September next to serve as Jurors, Viz Lorenzo Hunter, Wm Means, David W Barnet, Wm Gray, Alexander Cooper, Batte Irwin, J.J. Berryhill, Charles T Alexander, Wm Brown, WG Philips, Charles T Means, James Wallace Sr., Robert A McNeely, John G. Maxwell, Wilson N Miller, Wm Rea, F.H. Maxwell, David M Henderson, Wm Stinson, James N Ross, Thomas Gibson, Samuel Flanniken, Jas B Robinson, Robert Ormand, Robert H Young, Wm Hutchinson, George Campbell, E.C. Wallace, Wm Lee, A.R. Erwin, Jonathan Lewis, Tobias Wolf, G.C. Cathey, John Kirk Senr., Samuel B Hull, Joseph N. Rhyne. Herein fail not and have you then and there this Venire Facias.
    Witness B Oates, Clerk of the Court of pleas & Quarter Sessions for the County of Mecklenburg the 4th Monday of July AD 1853.
B. Oates, Clk
Which Venire Facias is Endorsed
Executed, T.N. Alexander, Shff

And of the said persons so Summoned the following were Called and drawn as a Grand Jury to inquire for the State and for the body of the said County to wit. James N Ross 1, John G. Maxwell 2, E.C. Wallace 3, DM Henderson 4, George Campbell 5, William Rea 6, David W Barnet 7, Samuel Flanniken 8, James B. Robinson 9, Wm Means 10, AR Erwin 11,

Iredell County
Criminal Actions

Lorenzo Hunter 12, Wm Lee 13, Joseph N. Rhyne 14, Jonathan Lewis 15, Robert A. McNeely 16, Saml. B. Hall 17, and GC Cathey 18.

His Honor the Judge appointed William Rea Foreman, and the Said Jurors being all Called and duly Sworn and Empannelled as the Grand Inquest for the body of said County of Mecklenburg and charged by the Judge; It is presented by the Jurors as follows to wit;

State of North Carolina   } Superior Court of Law
Mecklenburg County   } Fall Term 1853

   The Jurors for the State upon their Oath Present that Tom, a person of Color and a Slave, the property of Robert F Davidson, late of the County of Mecklenburg on the tenth day of September in the year of our Lord one thousand Eight hundred & fifty three with force and arms at and in the County aforesaid in and upon one Mary A. Gribble (a white Female) in the peace of God and the State then and there being violently and Feloniously did make an assault, and her the said Mary A Gribble, then and there, did beat wound and ill treat with intention her the said Mary A. Gribble violently and against her will then and there feloniously to ravish and carnally know and other wrongs to the Said Mary A. Gribble then and there did to the great damage of the said Mary A Gribble Contrary to the form of the Statute in Such Case made and provided and against the peace and dignity of the State.
Sander, Sol.
The following witnesses were Sworn and sent, to wit.
"William Gribble   } Witnesses
Mary A. Gribble   }
Sworn & sent
JB Kerr, Clk"

Which said Bill of Indictment is Endorsed
"A True Bill"
William Rea, Foreman

State Vs Tom (a Slave)

   Process Waived, Notice admitted by Robert F. Davidson the owner of the defendant. And the said Tom a person of Color and a Slave the property of R F Davidson is brought to the Bar of the Court here in his proper person by the Said Thomas N. Alexander, Sheriff of Mecklenburg

Iredell County
Criminal Actions

County in whose Custody he is. He is therefore again Committed to the Custody of the Sheriff and Said Indictment being Read to the said Defendant and forthwith it being demanded of him how he will acquit himself of the premises in the said Indictment above Specified and Charged upon him he saith he is not guilty thereof and thereof for good & for Evil he puts himself upon the Country and Wm Sander Esqr Solicitor who prosecutes for the State doth the like -- Whereupon the following affidavit is offered by Robert F Davidson the owner of the defendant. To Wit.

State Vs Tom (a Slave)
Superior Court of Law, Fall Term 1853

Robert F. Davidson the owner of the defendant in the Case maketh Oath that he is advised & believes that much Excitement & prejudice Exist in the County of Mecklenburg against the defendant in this Case that the Subject of the Prosecution has been much Canvassed and that Such is the State of Public Sentiment that he does not believe he can have a fair Trial in this County.
Sworn to in open Court, R.F. Davidson
Novr 15/53, J.B. Kerr, Clk

Open the foregoing affidavit and a Motion to remove the Cause -- It is ordered by the Court that this Cause be removed to Iredell County for Trial. And it is further ordered that the Sheriff of Mecklenburg County deliver the Defendant to the Sheriff of Iredell County on Wednesday after the 4th Monday in March next.

State Of North Carolina } Superior Court of Law
Mecklenburg County   }

I Jennings B Kerr Clerk of the Superior Court of Law of Said County do hereby Certify that the forgoing Transcript contains a true and perfect copy of the Record in the Case therein recited.

In Testimony whereof I have hereunto set my hand and affixed the Seal of said Court at Office this 28 September 1854.
JB Kerr, Clk SC

Iredell County
Criminal Actions

On the tenth of September in the year 1853 a slave named Tom, the property of R.F. Davidson, of Mecklenburg County, N.C. was accused of Rape by a white woman named Mary A. Gribble.

When questioned about the accusation the slave Tom pleaded not guilty. A Grand Jury was selected and a True Bill of Indictment was returned.

The Trial drew so much attention that Robert F. Davidson, the owner of the Slave Tom, protested and stated that Tom could not have a fair Trial in the County of Mecklenburg.

As a result the Trial was moved to Iredell County, N.C., and the slave Tom was transferred by the Sheriff to the jail in Statesville. Again Tom pleaded not guilty. For some reason the proceedings of the Trial and the Transcript were questioned by the Morgan District Court. It was, however, decided that the proceedings were in order.

Although Subpoenas were issued, and witnesses were called for both the State and the Plaintiff, no testimony has been found to date.

The Slave Tom was ordered to be executed on the 2nd day of November in the year 1855.

Judgment

"The Judgment of the Court is that Tom, a Slave, the prisoner at the bar, be taken to the prison from whence he came and from thence to the place of execution on Friday the second day of November next ensuing, and there between the hours of 10 oClock in the forenoon and 4 oClock in the afternoon of the same day be hanged by the neck until he be dead."

****

State Vs. Rufus, a Slave
Criminal Actions
Theft
Iredell County, NC [1855]

State of North Carolina   } To any lawful Officer
Iredell County   } of said County

Whereas information has been made to me one of the acting Justices of the Peace of the County and State aforesaid that a Negro boy

Iredell County
Criminal Actions

named Rufus, a Slave, the property of Thomas Summers has had and has now has in his possession a Twenty and a ten Dollar bill, Which it is believed he came by dishonestly & is the property of M. Campbell or some person unknown.

This is thereupon to command you to apprehend the said Rufus and him safely keep so you have him before me or some Other Justice of the Peace of said County to be further dealt with as the law directs. Fail not, given under my hand and seal this [Smudged] June 1855.
Silas D Sharpe,   JP
WF Cowan,   JP
Inst. Subp., in $100 - issue Subp., Bond is 100

Summons the State
Thos. J. Robb, Amos Jacobs, Mary Ann Johnson & M Campbell.

State of North Carolina   } June 9th 1855
Iredell County   }

After maturely investigating this Case it is adjudged that the said Slave Rufus is guilty of the charge and that the office further investigation deserves [Inserted sentence, unclear in meaning] & other punishment and that the said Slave be commited or give security for his appearance at the next Court of pleas and Quarter Sessions to be held in the town of Statesville in the County of Iredell On the 3rd Monday in August next and there to abide the decision of said Court. Given under my hand & seal the day & year above written.
W.F. Cowan, JP   (Seal)

State Vs Rufus, a Slave, the property of Thos. Summers
Executed by R.L. Willson, Constable

Thomas Summers bound in the sum of two hundred dollars as the Security for his Slave Rufus appearance at the Court above recited.
Thomas Summers

Witnesses for the State, Amos Jacobs, bound in $100, Mary Ann Johnson do $100.
Before me
WF Cowan, JP   (Seal)

Iredell County
Criminal Actions

State Vs Rufus, a Slave
Evidence
State Vs Rufus (a Slave) belonging to Thos Summers

Coln Campbell Being duly Sworn Says the day he surveyed a peas of Land for Thomas Summers & G.W. Chiply he left his coat packets [?] on the fence Leading to Thomas Summers Barn & that after getting home he Locked his Packet [?] he thinks there was between thirty & forty Dollars missing. That hearing of the boy Rufus the property of Thomas Summers being in possession of large bills of money he Examined said Boy Rufus in the presence of his Master as to where he got a ten dollar & a twenty dollar bills which it was reported he had, he Rufus Stated that he got the Ten dollar bill in Change for a twenty dollar bill from Amos Jacobs. That he got the twenty dollar bill from Mrs. Mary Ann Johnson wife of Amos Johnson. He also Stated that Mr. Jacobs gave him a five dollar & a three[?] dollar bill - with the ten dollar bill - above aluded to Mr Amos Jacobs Being Sworn Says he Changed a Twenty Dollar Bill for Rufus the Slave in question by Amos Johnson order which order was produced, he further Says he does not Recolect the amount he paid the Boy in Change for the said twenty Dollar Bill, neither does he recolect whether the Boy Said the Bill was his or not.
Not Cross Examined by Summers.

Marry Ann Johnson Being Sworn Says she never Saw the Twenty Dollar Bill in Question But admits She wrote an order to Amos Jacobs to Change the Bill for Rufus the slave in question & signed Amos Johnson Name to the order further she does not no where the money belonged too, She wrote the order at the Time it is dated. She further States she never Loaned him any money at any Time.
Not cross Examined by Summers.

Sn   Amos Jacobs
Recaled by Plff

On his Oath that the Twenty Dollar Bill was first Brought to him to get changed by [?] a Slave Belonging to Franklin Hause he refused to change it because he thought it to be counterfeit & Retained it until Rufus

Iredell County
Criminal Actions

the Slave in question Brought & order from Amos Johnson the one produced or [?] he had the Bill some Two or three weaks in his possession.

State Vs. Rufus (a Slave) of Thomas Summers
Subp. For the State, To Fall Term 1855
Executed, H Troutman, Shff
By W.F. Wasson

State of North Carolina
To the Sheriff of Iredell County - Greetings:
    You are hereby commanded to Summon Mary Ann Johnson personally to be and appear before the Judge of our Superior Court of Law, at the next Court to be held for our said County, at the Court-House in Statesville on the 6th Monday after the 4th Monday in Augt. Next; then and there to testify, and the truth to say in behalf of the State Grand Jury in a certain matter of controversy before said Court depending, and then and there to be tried, wherein the State is Plaintiff and Rufus (a Slave) is Defendant.
    And this you shall in no wise omit, under the penalty prescribed by Law.
    Witness, C.S. Summers, Clerk of our said Court at Office, the 1st Monday after the 4th Monday in March 1855, and in the [Blank] year of our Independence.
C.S. Summers, Clk

State Vs. Rufus, a Slave
To Fall Term 1855
Executed, H. Troutman, Shff
By W.F. Wasson, DS

State of North Carolina
To the Sheriff of Iredell County-Greeting:
    You are hereby commanded to Summon Thomas J Robb & George W Chipley personally to be and appear before the Judge of our Superior Court of Law, at the next Court to be held for our said County, at the Court-House in Statesville on the 6th Monday after the 4th Monday in August next; then and there to testify, and the truth to say in behalf of the State in a certain matter of controversy before said Court depending, and

Iredell County Criminal Actions

then and there to be tried Wherein the State is Plaintiff and Rufus, a Slave the property of Thos. Summers is Defendant. And this you shall in no wise omit, under the penalty prescribed by Law.

Witness, C.S. Summers, Clerk of our said Court at Office, the 1st Monday after the 4th Monday in March 1855 and in the [Blank] year of our Independence.

C.S. Summers, Clk

State Vs. Rufus, a Slave
Subp, To Fall Term 1855
Executed, H. Troutman, Shff
By W.F. Wasson, JS

State of North Carolina
To the Sheriff of Iredell County-Greeting:

You are hereby commanded to Summon Hiram Summers, Thos. Summers, Amos Johnston personally to be and appear before the Judge of our Superior Court of Law, at the next Court to be held for our said County, at the Court House in Statesville on the 6th Monday after the 4th Monday in August next; then and there to testify, and the truth to say in behalf of Rufus, a Slave, in a certain matter of controversy before our said Court depending, and then and there to be tried, wherein the State is Plaintiff and Rufus a Slave is Defendant. And this you shall in no wise omit, under the penalty prescribed by Law.

Witness, C.S. Summers, Clerk of our said Court at Office, the 1st Monday after the 4th Monday in March 1855, and in the 79th year of our Independence.

C.S. Summers, Clk

State Vs. Rufus, a Slave
Transcript
To Fall Term 1855

4 Recognizances	80
Transcript	2.00
	2.80

State of North Carolina }

Iredell County
Criminal Actions

Iredell County }

Be it remembered that at a Court of Pleas & Quarter Sessions begun & held for the County of Iredell at the Court-House in Statesville on the 3rd Monday of August A.D. 1855 before Thomas A Allison, John H. McLaughlin & John Davidson, Justices of said Court. R.L. Wilson, Constable returned into Court a State Warrant against Rufus, a Slave, the property of Thomas Summers, (Which warrant is herewith sent) Thereupon the following record is made.

State Vs Rufus, a Slave of Thomas Summers

Thomas Summers the owner of Rufus bound in $400 for his appearance at the next Superior Court of Law for Iredell County. M. Campbell, W.F. Cowan and Amos Jacobs bound each $100.

State of North Carolina } J. Milas F. Freeland
Iredell County }

Clerk of the Court of Pleas & Quarter Sessions for said County & State do hereby certify that the foregoing is a True & Perfect transcript of the record of said Court in the case of the State against Rufus, a Slave.

In Testimony whereof I have hereunto set my hand & affixed the Seal of said Court at Office the 8th day of October A.D. 1855.
M.F. Freeland, Clk

****

State Vs. Marlow
Criminal Actions
Assisting a Slave to Escape
Iredell County, NC [1855]

State Vs Marlow
Subp. Inst., Spring 1856
Executed, H Trautman, Shff
By W.F. Wasson

State of North Carolina
To the Sheriff of Iredell County-Greeting:

Iredell County
Criminal Actions

You are hereby commanded to Summon Wm F Stone personally to be and appear before the Judge of our Superior Court of Law, at the next Court to be held for our said County, at the Court-House in Statesville on the 6th Monday after the 4th Monday in Inst; then and there to testify, and the truth to say in behalf of the State in a certain matter the Grand Jury depending, and then and there to be Tried, wherein the State is Plaintiff and Wm P Marlow is Defendant. And this you shall in no wise omit, under the penalty prescribed by Law.

Witness, C S Summers, Clerk of our said Court, at Office, the 6th Monday after the 4th Monday in Fall 1856, and in the 80th year of our Independence.
CS Summers, Clk

State Vs. Marlow, Subp.
To Spring Term 1856
Executed, G, Shff

State of North Carolina
To the Sheriff of Wilkes County-Greetings:

You are hereby commanded to Summon John Oatsman personally to be and appear before the Judge of our Superior Court of Law, at the next Court to be held for our said County, at the Court-House in Statesville on the 6th Monday after the 4th Monday Feby next; then and there to testify, and the truth to say in behalf of Wm P Marlow in a certain matter of controversy before said Court, depending, and then and there to be tried, wherein the State is Plaintiff and Wm P Marlow is Defendant. And this you shall in no wise omit, under the penalty prescribed by Law.

Witness CS Summers, Clerk of our said Court at Office, the 6th Monday after the 4th Monday in Augt 1855, and in the 80th year of our Independence.
C.S. Summers, Clk

State Vs Wm P Marlow
Subp, to Spring Term 1856
Not to be found, H Troutman, Shff
To Hand this 15th March 1856

State of North Carolina.

Iredell County
Criminal Actions

To the Sheriff of Iredell County-Greeting:

You are hereby Commanded to Summon Mary Marlow personally to be and appear before the Judge of our Superior Court of Law, at the next Court to be held for our said County, at the Court-House in Statesville on the 6th Monday after the 4th Monday in Feby next; then and there to testify, and the truth to say in behalf of Wm P Marlow in a certain matter of controversy before said Court depending, and then and there to be Tried, wherein the State is Plaintiff and Wm P. Marlow is Defendant. And this you shall in no wise omit, under the penalty prescribed by Law.

Witness, C.S. Summers, Clerk of our said Court, at Office, the 6th Monday after the 4th Monday in Augt 1855, and in the 80th year of our Independence.

C.S. Summers, Clk

Wm P Marlow Vs the County

Indictment	.60
Certificate	.20
3 Subp	.43
1 Seal & Postage	.28
Judgment & Bill	1.10
Jury	.10
D. Wilson	.30
E Stayley	.30
	3.33
	1.66 1/2
H E Allen	2.62
W F Stone	1.54
R J Johnson	2.18
Thos W [?]	2.70
Thos Radiner	2.06
	12.76 1/2
105.85	150.16
26.46	
132.31	152.31
6	15.97
793.86	2.8
793.86	

Iredell County
Criminal Actions

1597.72
<u>198</u>
17.95 Inters. For 2 years & 3 months
<u>132.97</u>
150.92

Examination of the Witnesses
State Vs Wm P. Marlow

Silas Keaton Witness for the State, he says he or was found a pass in the possession of boy Thorton which is a forged pass from Information, led me to suspicion sd Marlow and got him to do some hand riting and then compareing the pass & the hand riting I saw him rite and he thinks & believes that there is a similarity of the two that is one person rote them both
Silas Keaton

Thos W Redman for the State being sworn saith that in comparing the pass & the balance of his hand riting that the two have a striking resemblance of each other sworn to & subscribed.
T.W. Redman

H.E. Allen for the State saith after I saw him rite and the pass he thinks & believes that one person rote them both, sworn & subscribed.
H.E. Allen

Thos Redman for the State saith after viewing the riting he said he Marlow rote & the pass he says there is some resemblance to each other, Sworn & Subscribed
Thos Redman

RM Johnson for the State saith after seeing Marlow Rite then comparing the pass & his riting that they have a striking resemblance, Sworn & Subscribed
R.M. Johnson

State Vs Wm. P. Marlow

Iredell County
Criminal Actions

For the want of a lawful officer I deputize R M Johnson. Summon for the State S. Keaton, Thos Redman, T.W. Redman, H E Allen & R.M. Johnson.

Summon for Defendant ~~Thos W. Redmon~~

State Of North Carolina }
Iredell County }

    Whereas this day came Silas Keaton before me one of the acting Justices of the Peace in and for said County and made oath in due form of law that he has in his possession a written free pass found in the hands of a negro boy Thornton which pass he has good reason to believe that Pleasant Marlow did rite and give to sd boy belonging to Jos. Grey according to the comparison of his riting with the pass much against the peace and dignity of the State.
    These are therefore to command you to take the body of Wm P Marlow if to be found in your County and have him before me or some other Justice of the Peace in sd County to answer the aforesaid charge and be further dealt with according to law. Herein fail not, given under my hand and seal the 13th day of February 1856.
H.E. Allen, JP SC

State Vs Wm. P. Marlow
Indict. Assisting a Slave to escape from his owner
Nol - Pros

Witnesses, Silas Keaton, H.E. Allen, R.M. Johnson & WF Stone
Sworn & Sent, C S Summers, Clk. A True Bill, M Campbell, Foreman.

North Carolina } Superior Court of Law
Iredell County } Spring Term 1856

    The jurors for the State upon their oath present that WP Marlow on the 19th of October 1855 with force and arms in the County aforesaid unlawfully did entice, pursuade and tempt a certain negro slave named Thornton the property of one Joseph Gray to absent himself from his owners service by writing for and delivering to the said Slave Certain false forged and Counterfeited Certificates which said Certificates among other things falsely alleged that said Slave was a free man born of a free Colored

Iredell County
Criminal Actions

woman, and by other unlawful means; And the Jurors aforesaid upon their oath aforesaid do further present that W.P. Marlow on the day & year aforesaid in the County aforesaid, unlawfully did harbor and maintain a Certain negro Slave named Thornton the property of one Joseph Gray, during and while the said negro was runaway from his said owner, Contrary to the form of the statute in such case made and provided and against the peace and dignity of the State.
Sander, Sol.

****

State Vs. Andrew Kerr
Criminal Actions
Trading with Slaves
Iredell County, NC [1856]

State Vs. Andrew Kerr
Subp. For State, to Fall Term 1856

Executed on R.S Gillespie, R. Brown, Ephraim Scroggs not to be found, & H. Troutman, Shff

State of North Carolina
To the Sheriff of Iredell County - Greeting:
    You are hereby Commanded to Summon Robert Brown, Robert L. Gillespie & Ephraim Scroggs personally to be and appear before the Judge of our Superior Court of Law, at the next Court to be held for our said County, at the Court-House in Statesville on the 6th Monday after the 4th Monday in August next; then and there testify, and the truth to say in behalf of the State in a certain matter of controversy before said Court depending, and then and there to be Tried, wherein the State is Plaintiff and Andrew Kerr is Defendant. And this you shall in no wise omit, under the penalty prescribed by Law.
    Witness, C.S. Summers, Clerk of our said Court at Office, the 6th Monday after the 4th Monday in **[Blank]** 1856, and in the **[Blank]** year of our Independence.
C S Summers. Clk

State Vs Andrew Kerr

Iredell County
Criminal Actions

Appeal to Fall Term 1856

A. Kerr to answer bound $400. A. Troutman, R.S. Mills, Levi Vanderburg & George W Kerr bound as securities Jointly, $400.

State of North Carolina }
Iredell County }

  Be it remembered that at a Court of Pleas & Quarter Sessions begun & held for the County of Iredell; at the Court House in Statesville on the 3rd Monday in February A.D. 1856 before John H. McLauglin, John Davidson, T.A. Allison & M. Campbell, Justices of said Court, upon the oath of:
1. A.R. Morrison, 2. Thomas S. Brown, 3. H.E. Robison, 4. [?] Cash, 5. James A. Watts, 6. Wm Myers, Foreman, 7. Hiel L. Poston, 8. W.F. House, 9. R.M. Johnston, 10. W.L. Westmoreland, 11. Dempsey Woodward, 12. M.W. Milligan, 13. J.W. Long, 14. Silas A. McEwen, 15. Joseph Allison, good and lawful men of the County aforesaid, duly summoned drawn, Sworn, & charged, to inquire for the State of and concerning all crimes and offences committed within the body of the said County, it is presented in manner & form following, that is to say:

North Carolina } Court of Pleas & Quarter
Iredell County } Sessions Feb Term 1856

  The Jurors for the State upon their oaths present that Andrew Kerr, laborer, late of said County on the first day of February A.D. 1856, in the County aforesaid, did unlawfully buy of, and receive from Nelson, a Slave, the property of Robert C. Brown a certain quantity of wheat, to wit, one bushel the said Slave, then & there not having the permission in writing of his owner, Master or person having control of him, to sell & deliver the said wheat to the said Andrew Kerr; contrary to the form of the Statute in such case made & provided and against the peace & dignity of the State.
R.M. Allison, Sol.

  Whereupon the Sheriff of said County is Commanded that he cause the said Andrew Kerr to come & answer; and afterwards, to wit on the 3rd Monday in August A.D. 1856 before John H McLaughlin, John Davidson & M. Campbell, Justices of said Court, cometh the said Andrew

Iredell County
Criminal Actions

Kerr in his own proper person, & having heard the said Indictment read, he, the said Andrew Kerr, saith that he is not guilty thereof, and of this he puts himself upon the County, and R.M. Allison, County Solicitor who prosecutes for the State doth the like. Therefore lat a Jury come of good & lawful men by whom the truth of the matter may be better known. And thereupon the following Jurors, to Wit.
1. Ephraim Templeton, 2. Wm J. Holland, 3. John E. Poston, 4. Benjamin Atwell, 5. Ivy Gaither, 6. Thomas W. Tomlinson, 7. James Fletcher, 8. John F. McLean, 9. James Tucker, 10. D.W. Holman, 11. Leander Gaither, 12. Benjamin Mundy being chosen & Sworn to speak the truth of and concerning the premises, in the said Indictment specified, do say upon their oath that the said Andrew is guilty thereof in manner & form as charged in the Bill of Indictment. And it is thereupon considered by the Court that the said Andrew Kerr be imprisoned ten days & pay the costs of suit.

From the above Judgment the said Andrew Kerr prays an appeal to the Superior Court of Law of Iredell County and it is allowed to him, upon his giving bond with A. Troutman, R.L. Mills, Levi Vanderburg & George W. Kerr as sureties. Said Bond is executed in Open Court & is herewith sent.

Indictment	.60
Tax	1.00
5 Recognizances	1.00
1 Certificate	.20
Judgment & Bill	1.10
Solicitor	4.00
	7.90
Appeal Bond	.60
Transcript & Seal	1.25
Appeal Tax	.80
R.L. Gillespie	3.56
	14.11

  I, M.F. Freeland, Clerk of the Court of Pleas & Quarter Sessions of the County & State aforesaid do hereby certify that the foregoing contains a full, true & perfect transcript of the record in the said Indictment.
  In Testimony whereof I have hereunto set my hand and affixed the seal of my Office at Office in Statesville the 6th day of October A.D. 1856.

Iredell County
Criminal Actions

M F Freeland, Clk

State of North Carolina } Superior Court of Law
Iredell County } Fall Term, 1856

In the Suit of, State Versus Andrew Kerr

R.C. Brown charges the State in this cause for attendance as a witness, 2
days at 60 per day   1.20
Mileage to Court & home, 16 miles   .32
Ferriage, this Ticket   .10
    1.62

State of North Carolina } Superior Court of Law
Iredell County } Fall Term, 1856

In the Suit of, State versus Andrew Kerr

R S Gillespie charges the State in this cause for attendance as a witness, 2
days at 60 per day.   1.20
Mileage to Court and home, 24 miles   .48
Ferriage, this Ticket   .10
    1.78

Sworn to before me, at Office, the 7th day of Octr 1856
C.S. Summers, Clk

State Vs Andrew Kerr
Bill of Costs

Indictment	.60
Tax	1.00
5 Recognizances	1.00
1 Certificate	.20
Judgment & Bill	1.10
Solicitor	4.00
Appeal Bond	.60

Iredell County
Criminal Actions

Transcript & Seal	1.25
Appeal Tax	.80
R.S. Gillespie	3.56
County Court Costs	14.11
Superior Court Cost Fine	10.00
Docketing Appeal	1.00
1 Subp	.15
Judgment & Bill	1.10
Shff	.90
Solicitor	4.00
R.S. Gillespie	1.78
1 recognizance	.20
	33.24
Robt Brown	1.62
	34.86

****

State Vs. Wilson, a Slave
Criminal Actions
Murder
Iredell County, NC [1858]

B B Lunday States that Wilson the prisoner showed him a bill on last Saturday morning between 8 & 9 O'clock, which he said his master gave him & that he had forgot how much it was that he told him it was a five dollar Bill, which bill he thinks was on the Bank of Cape Fear and appeared quite new.

F. Sanders - Wm Jones, B B Lunday, R.M. Johnson, John Brawley & Allison Freeland bound for the appearance of Edmund Each in the sum of one hundred dollars to be & appear at the Court House in the town of Statesville on **[Faded]** the 4th day of October next & give Evidence in behalf of the State against Wilson.

M. Campbell, JP
J E Summers, JP   (Seal)

State of North Carolina }

Iredell County
Criminal Actions

Iredell County   }

Whereas Wilson (a Slave the property of Nancy Allison) being brought before us, charged with breaking and Robbing the house of Margaret Freeland and Committing a violent assault and battery upon the body of the said Margaret Freeland with intention to murder her.

The said Wilson Confesses that he went to the House of the said Margaret who lived alone, in Company with Isaac, a Slave the property of A. Weber on the [Faded] that the door was locked, that after some prying he Isaac forced the door - and went in (pulling) the door too after him, that he herd her Holler Repeatedly, that the [?] not from the house for a time before he came out. She ceased to holler but that he still herd her groan; That Isaac then came out through the window, that Isaac gave him a bill which he passed to Mr. Jones on the Saturday following, which bill, he was told was a five dollar bill, that he brought a pair of shoes, a Calico dress & a pr. Of pantaloons from Mr Jones and gave him the five dollar bill & 4 quarters in Silver - That Isaac told him he had about [?] dollars left. Which he took off with and that he has not seen Isaac since. William Jones testified that the boy Wilson came to his Store in the forenoon on Saturday last that he gave him a five dollar bill and five quarters in Silver for which he gave him goods, a dress & shoes

Edmund a Slave of Nancy Allison, brother to Wilson after being Charged and Sworn Says that Wilson & him generally Sleep in the same bed. That on Thursday night Wilson did not come to bed as usual but laid down on the floor and he went to Sleep and left him there, I saw him no more until Friday morning - and then he had changed his Clothes - and had on Clean Clothes, that their Mother asked Wilson why he put on his Clean Clothes at that time of the week. That Wilson gave her no answer - That Wilson was gone on Saturday from about nine O'Clock until Twelve - That Wilson told him he was out on Thursday night with a fellow but did not tell who the fellow was nor where they were. Les a Slave the Property of Franklin House being Sworn says that on Sunday night after the alarm was given of Mrs. Freelands situation. That he was in company with Edmund - that he told him he was at Mrs. Freelands house on Saturday and that the door was chained but not Locked and that he went home and told it but did not say who he told it too.

Wilson further Says that Isaac had a Staff with a Spear in the [?] End. That the Spear was sharp on two sides at this End, which was covered with a cap - That Isaac told him he thought he had killed Mrs. Freeland

Iredell County
Criminal Actions

M Franklin Freland first found the dec'd. wounded on Sunday the 1st of Aug- at Night on the Saturday after it happened, the prisoner, went to B B Lundy, and showed him a book note and asked him what it was: he said his young Master Franklin Allison gave it him, he had forgotten how much it was. John M Branley knew she had money on Munday the 2nd, prisoner was taken up - after some confessions as to one Isaac a Slave of Adam Webber had gone in & he had stayed at the farm, he was then taken with the guard to Saml Chamberlains[?] before he went to [?] he stated the place in a branch where Webbers negro worked the blood from his hands about 60 or 50 yards from the house, blood was found in the branch: he on next day he said he was in the house with Webbers negro on Wednesday in jail after the Gol[?] was found. M.F. Freland with R.C. Chambers, AB Kilpatrick & M. Gurney, H McLocklin went to the jail and after some talk Freland said we have the $20 or the balance of the money, Webbers negro could not have any of the money, & we now know all about it & you might as well tell the truth, this will be a solemn matter for you & you had better make your peace with your God. He [?] and then said he would tell the truth, that Webbers negro was not there, that he had gone in the house by himself & found her asleep, that he went to the Chest and got the pocket book before he waked her, he then went to the bed & put his hand on her breast, she moved & he struck her with the stick & that he cut her with the knife, she said the Lord have Mercy on me, he thought she was dead, he then went to the branch & washed, he crossed the branch went down the spring branch & threw the stick over the fence in the woods - the place the stick was found by Kilpatrick & Chambers.

    On another occasion on the day of the election or about that time Wilson, Gurney & Saml Dockery went to the jail, and inquired about the pocket book, he told them where he [?] half that had the strap, they found it at the place mentioned, and near the same place the receipt tore up. He said the other half was in the Kitchen and it was found there by Thomas Gourney & James M. Gurney.

    The Pocket book is identified by JM Branley and the receipt by Silas Keaton, Jacob Fraley & Joshua Dowell proves Declarations in the jail afterwards FM Sanders to dec'd. home on Wednesday night before she was found.

Statesville, Oct 22nd 1858

Iredell County Criminal Actions

Allison Freeland Dr
To Jas H McLaughlin Jailor

For boy Wilson jail fees 81 days at .40 per day	$32.40
To Reg. Fees at .30 Each time	4.50
To blankets	7.60
	$44.50
To assessing to take Wilsons measure for Coffin	.30
	$44.80

Wilsons Act.
$44.80
$44.80

State Vs Wilson a Slave
Notice to Owners, to Fall 1858
Executed, W.F. Wasson, Shff
By W. Gurney, Dp.

State of North Carolina
To the Sheriff of Iredell County, Greetings:
You are hereby commanded to notify Miss Nancy Allison, W.A. Freeland and M. Franklin Freeland that at a Superior Court of Law to be held for said County at the Court House in Statesville on the 6th Monday after the 4th Monday in August 1858. Wilson, a Slave the property of Miss Nancy Allison will be put upon Trial for his Life -- charged with the murder of Mrs. Margaret Freeland Dec'd. when & where they can attend & defend said slave if they see proper. And this you shall in no wise omit.
Issued, 9 September 1858
R.A. McLaughlin, CSC

State Vs. Wilson, a Slave
Subp for State, to Fall 1858
Executed, Dr. Lang, M. Laughlin
A. Freeland & C. Chambers
P.C. Carlton

Iredell County
Criminal Actions

Executed & am, Daniel Feraby
W.F. Wasson, Shff
Executed, W.F. Wasson, Shff
By W.A. Gurney

State of North Carolina
To the Sheriff of Iredell County - Greeting:
  You are hereby commanded to Summon Wm. F. Cowan, Jacob Fraley, Joshua Dowell, Cowan Chambers, Saml. Dockery, James McLaughlin, Dr. Lang, Dr. R.T. Campbell, Wilson Gurney, A.B. Kilpatrick, W.A. Freeland, M. Franklin Freeland, & Andrew Freeland Jr., personally to be and appear before the Judge of our Superior Court of Law, at the next Court to be held for our said County, at the Court-House in Statesville, on the 6th Monday after the 4th Monday in August, then and there to testify, and the truth to say in behalf of the State in a certain matter of controversy before said Court depending, and then and there to be Tried, wherein the State is Plaintiff and Wilson a Slave the property of Nancy Allison is Defendant. And this you shall in no wise omit, under the penalty prescribed by Law.
  Witness -- R.A. McLaughlin, Clerk of our said Court, at Office, the 6th Monday after the 4th Monday in Feby 1858. And in the **[Blank]** year of our Independence.
Issued 9 Sept. 1858
R.A. McLaughlin, CSC

State Vs. Wilson, a Slave
Subp Instanter
Executed, W.F. Wasson, Shff

State of North Carolina
To the Sheriff of the County, Greeting:
  You are hereby Commanded to Summon Wm S. House personally to be and appear before the Judge of our Superior Court of Law, at the next Court to be held for our said County, at the Court-House in Statesville, on the 6th Monday after the 4th Monday in August Instanter, then and there to testify, and the truth to say in behalf **[?]** in a certain matter of controversy before said Court depending, and then and there to be Tried, wherein the State is Plaintiff and Wilson, a Slave is Defendant. And this you shall in no wise omit, under the penalty prescribed by law.

Iredell County
Criminal Actions

Witness -- R.A. McLaughlin, Clerk of our said Court, at Office, the 6th Monday after the 4th Monday in **[Blank]** and in the **[Blank]** year of our Independence.
R.A. McLaughlin, Clk.

Rec'd of R.A. McLaughlin One Dollar & fifty two cents for my attendance as a Witness in case of State Vs. Wilson a Slave.
3d Nov 1858
R.C. Chambers

State Vs. Wilson, a Slave
Subp Instanter, Fall Term 1858
Executed, W.F. Wasson, Shff

State of North Carolina
To the Sheriff of **[Blank]** County - Greeting:
  You are hereby Commanded to Summon Wm. M. Allison, Thomas Gurney & James M. Gurney personally to be and appear before the Judge of our Superior Court of Law, at the next Court to be held for our said County, at the Court-House in Statesville, on the 6th Monday after the 4th Monday in August Instanter, then and there to testify, and the truth to say in behalf of the State in a certain matter of controversy before said Court depending, and then and there to be Tried, wherein the State is Plaintiff and Wilson, a Slave is Defendant. And this you shall in no wise omit, under the penalty prescribed by Law.
  Witness -- R.A. McLaughlin, Clerk of our said Court, at Office, the 6th Monday after the 4th Monday in August 1858 and in the 83rd year of our Independence.
R.A. McLaughlin, Clk

State Vs. Wilson, a Slave
Subp Instanter
Executed, W.F. Wasson, Shff

State of North Carolina
To the Sheriff of Iredell County - Greeting:
  You are Hereby Commanded to Summon Silas Keaton personally to be and appear before the Judge of our Superior Court of Law, at the next

Iredell County Criminal Actions

Court to be held for our said County, at the Court-House in Statesville, on the 6th Monday after the 4th Monday in August Inst. Then and there to testify, and the truth to say in behalf of the State in a certain matter of controversy before said Court depending, and then and there to be Tried, wherein the State is Plaintiff and Wilson, a Slave, is the Defendant. And this you shall in no wise omit, under the penalty prescribed by Law.

   Witness - R.A. McLaughlin, Clerk of our said Court, at Office, the 6th Monday after the 4th Monday in Augt. 1858, and in the 83rd year of our Independence.
R.A. McLaughlin, Clk

State Vs. Wilson (a Slave)
Indt. Murder
Gov Pros

A True Bill
John Templeton, Foreman

Anderson Freeland, Thos. [?], James M Lowry, Wm M Allison, Silas Rector 1858

M. Campbell	+
R.C. Chambers	+
AB Kilpatrick	+
Wilson [?]	+
Saml. Dockery	+
Dr. J.F. Long	+
Dr. R.T. Campbell	+
Wm. F. Cowan	+
M.F. Freland	E+
Jacob Fraley	+
+M. Franklin Freland	E+
W.A. Freland	+
Francis M. Saunders	+
W.B. Jones	+
R.M. Johnson	
J.M. Branley	+
+Edmund (a Slave)	+
Joshua [?]	+

Iredell County
Criminal Actions

Those marke E those + Sworn & Sent
R.A. McLaughlin, Clk

North Carolina } Superior Court of Law
Iredell County } Fall Term 1858

  The Jurors for the State upon their oath present that Wilson, a slave the property of Nancy Allison, not having the fear of God before his eyes but being moved and seduced by the instigation of the devil on the 29th day of July in the year of our Lord one thousand eight hundred and fifty-eight with force and arms, in the County aforesaid, in and upon one Margaret Freeland in the peace of God, and the State, then & there being, feloniously, wilfully and of his malice aforethought, did make an assault; And that the said Wilson, a Slave as aforesaid, with a certain knife of the value of six pence which he the said Wilson in his right hand, then and there, had and held, the said Margaret Freland in and upon the left side of the throat and neck of her the said Margaret Freland, then and there, feloniously, wilfully, and of his malice aforethought, did strike and thrust, giving the said Margaret Freeland, then & there, with the knife aforesaid, in and upon her the said Margaret Freland one mortal wound of bredth of three inches and of the depth of six inches of which said mortal wound the said Margaret Freeland from the twenty ninth day of July in the year aforesaid, until the sixth day of August in the year aforesaid, in the County aforesaid, did languish, and languishing did live; on which said sixth day of August in the year aforesaid, the said Margaret Freeland in the County aforesaid of the said Mortal wound died; And so the jurors aforesaid upon their oath aforesaid, do say that the said Wilson, a Slave, (the property of one Nancy Allison) the said Margaret Freland in manner and from aforesaid feloniously, wilfully, and of his Malice aforethought did kill and Murder: Against the peace & dignity of the State.
Sanders, Sol.

State Vs. Wilson, a Slave
Order of Execution
Executed Octr 28 1858
W.F. Wasson, Shff

Iredell County
Criminal Actions

State of N. Carolina } Sup Co. of Law
Iredell County } Fall Term 1858

In this case it is ordered & adjudged by the Court that the boy Wilson, a Slave, be kept by the Sheriff of this County in the common Jail thereof until Friday the 22nd inst. When he shall be taken by the said Sheriff to the common place of execution for his County & between the hours of Ten O Clock in the morning and Two O'Clock in the afternoon, the said Sheriff shall hang him by the neck until this body be dead.
Witness R.A. McLaughlin, Clerk of our said Court at Office the 6th Monday after the 4th Monday in August AD 1858.
Issued 18th Oct 1858.
R.A. Mc Laughlin CSC

****

State vs. Amos Jacobs
Criminal Actions
Trading with Slaves
Iredell County, NC [1858]

North Carolina } Feb the 17th 1858
Iredell County }

To the honorable the Judge of the Superior Court of Law for the State aforesaid, your petitioner Amos Jacobs showeth unto your Honor that on the 4th day of February instant your petitioner was served with warrant by one Samuel Dockery for the penalty of one hundred dollars - in the charge of trading with a Slave the property of BC Altra by name of [?], that on the same day said warrant was returned before James Summers Esqr, a justice of the peace for said County - that a judgment was rendered against your petitioner for the sum of one hundred dollars & costs of the warrant - from which judgment your petitioner prayed an appeal to the County Court - and [?] ten days to give his sureties - That your petitioner as a very aged man - about Seventy years old - very infirm - and diseased, that his health was such that he could not without great risk and danger expose himself to cold and inclement weather - that your petitioner informed the magistrate that he would furnish sureties for his appeal by the last of next week - which would be in time. That your petitioner is a man of property - worth [?] one or two thousand dollars - that he owns a tract of

Iredell County
Criminal Actions

land worth one thousand dollars - and is clear of debt - that on the same day States warrant was tried for said offences & your petitioner not being ready with his sureties - was compelled for want thereof to go to jail that night - that he was not released untill next day by [?] sureties for his appearance - once at Court on States warrant - that your petitioner procured an aged lady by the name of Kilpatrick to go his surety for this appeal - and that she was to go on Friday or Saturday - following - that your petitioner was to go and take her to [?] - the magistrates - that Mrs Kilpatrick is an old and very infirm woman - that the said days Friday and Saturday - when they were to go to Esqr here with - for the said purpose - the weather was so very bad and inclement - by reason of a heavy fall of snow and hail on the Friday night and Saturday - your petitioner could not bear without great danger to his life - And that it would have him at the greatest risk of health and probably [?] to Mrs. Kilpatrick to have left home and gone to Mr Summers house.

    That on the account of the reasons above stated your petitioner failed to give the surety required by law for his appeal - that your petitioner is advised and believes that he has a good defense to said actions - and that he is intirely innocent of said charge.

    Your Petitioner therefore Prays that Honor grant unto him [?] commanding the said magistrate to make up in this cause to the next Superior Court of Law to be held for said County on this 6th Monday after the 4th Monday of February instant 1858 - And that noted thereof issue to the Plaintiff
Samuel Dockery

[?] Royden & W P Caldwell

Amos Jacobs the petitioner maketh oath that the facts set forth in this above petition as of his own knowledge are true and those not of his own knowledge he believes to be true
Febr 17th 1858
    His
Amos X Jacobs
    Mark

Sworn to before me - in testimony whereof I set my hand & seal of Office
M.F. Freeland, Clk

****

Iredell County Criminal Actions

State Vs. Bill Jones, a Free Negro
Criminal Actions
Assault & Battery
Iredell County, NC [1860]

State of North Carolina
Iredell County
To Jas H McLaughlin

To 107 days jail fees for Bill Jones a free boy at .40	$4280
To Key fees up & down .60	.60
To Blankets 143.40	8.40
For use of blanket 9.40	
[Faded] 152.80	

R.T. Summonton[?] for 4 years & 6 months for $152.80
26 May, [?]   4000.00
Statesville

State Vs. Bill Jones, a free Negro
Indictment and Battery, E   Pros.

Witnesses, + Dr. W.M. Campbell & + Independence, a Slave of MS [?]
Those Marked Thus +, sworn & sent
R.A. McLaughlin, Clk
A True Bill, W Summers

State of North Carolina   } Superior Court of Law
Iredell County   } Spring Term 1860

    The Jurors for the State, upon their oath present, that Bill Jones, a free Negro with force and arms, at and in the County aforesaid, on the 9th day of March A.D., 1860, in and upon the body of one Mary, a Slave of MA Wren in the peace of God, and the State then and there being, an assault did make, and the said Mary then and there did beat, wound, and ill treat, contrary to law, and against the peace and dignity of the State.

****

Iredell County Criminal Actions

State Vs. B.B. Lundy
Criminal Actions
Trading with Slaves
Iredell County, NC [1860]

State of North Carolina
To the Sheriff of Iredell County - Greeting:
    You are Hereby Commanded to Summon Jos Welsh & William Caughron, personally to be and appear before the next Court to be held for our said County, at the Court-House in Statesville, on the 6th Monday after the 4th Monday in Feby next; then and there to testify, and the truth to say in behalf of the State in a certain matter of controversy before said Court depending, and then and there to be Tried, wherein the State is Plaintiff and BBLundy is Defendant. And this you shall in no wise omit, under the penalty prescribed by Law.
    Witness **[Blank]** Clerk of our said Court, at Office, the 6th Monday after the 4th Monday in August 1859, and in **[Blank]** year of our Independence.
R.A. Mc Laughlin, CSC

North Carolina } Fall Term 1859
Iredell County }

    The Grand Jurors on their oath Present- B B Lundy for trading with Slaves.
Witness: Jos Welch, Wm Caughran
M Campbell, Foreman

State of North Carolina
To the Sheriff of Iredell County- Greeting:
    You are hereby Commanded to Summon Samuel Draky personally to be and appear before the Judge of our next Superior Court of Law, at the next Court to be held for our said County, at the Court-House on the 6th Monday after the 4th Monday in August next - then and there to testify, and the truth to say in behalf of the State in a certain matter of controversy in said Court depending, and then and there to be tried, Wherein the State is Plaintiff and BB Lundy is Defendant. And this you shall in no wise omit, under the penalty prescribed by Law.

Iredell County Criminal Actions

   Witness - RA McLaughlin, Clerk of our said Court, at Office, the 6th Monday after the 4th Monday in August, 18-- and in the **[Blank]** year of our Independence.
R.M. McLaughlin, CSC

State of North Carolina
To the Sheriff of Iredell County-Greeting:
   You are hereby Commanded to Summon Joseph Welch and Wm. Caughran personally to be and appear before the Judge of our next Superior Court of Law, at the next Court to be held for our said County, at the Court-House in Statesville on the 6th Monday after the 4th Monday in August next - then and there to testify, and the truth to say in behalf of the State in a certain matter of controversy in said Court Depending, and then and there to be Tried, wherein the State is Plaintiff and B.B. Lundy is Defendant. And this you shall in no wise omit, under the penalty prescribed by Law.
   Witness - RA McLaughlin, Clerk of our said Court, at Office, the 6th Monday after the 4th Monday in Feby 1860 and in the **[Blank]** year of our Independence.
R.A. Mc Laughlin, CSC

       State Vs. B.B. Lunday
        1860, Indictment
       Trading With Slaves

Joseph Welch +
Wm Caughran +
Saml Dockery
Those marked +, Sworn and Sent
R.A. McLaughlin, Clerk
A True Bill, W Turner, Foreman

State of North Carolina } Superior Court of Law
Iredell County   } Fall Term, 1860

Samuel Dockery In the Suit of; State Vs. B Lundy
Charges the X in this cause for attendance as a Witness

Iredell County
Criminal Actions

1 day at 60 per day   .60
Mileage to Court & home, 20 miles .40
Ferriage, this Ticket   .10
                                    1.10
Sworn to before me, at Office, the **[Blank]** day of **[Blank]**
RA McLaughlin, CSC

State of North Carolina   } Superior Court of Law
Iredell County   } Fall Term 1860

William Cockran In Suit of, State Vs. Lundy
Charges the X in this cause for attendance as a Witness
1 day at 60 per day   .60
Miles to Court & home, 20 miles   .40
Ferriage, this Ticket   .10
                                    1.10
Sworn to before me, at Office, the **[Blank]** day of **[Blank]**
RA McLaughlin, CSC

State of North Carolina   }Superior Court of Law
Iredell County   }Fall Term 1860

Joseph Welch In the Suit of, State Vs B Lundy
Charges the X in this cause for attendance as a Witness
1 day at 60 per day   .60
Miles to Court & home, 20 miles   .40
Ferriage, this Ticket   .10
                                    1.10

State of North Carolina   } Superior Court of Law
Iredell County   } Spring Term 1860

Wm Costner In the Suit of, State Vs Lunday
Charges the State in this cause for attendance as Witness
2 days at 60 per day   1.20
Miles to Court & home, 24 miles   .48
Ferriage, this Ticket   .10

Iredell County
Criminal Actions

1.78
Sworn to before me, at Office, the 10th day of Apr 1860
RA McLaughlin, CSC

State Vs. B B lundy

Tax	1.00
Judgment & Cost	1.10
Indt. & Bill	1.10
Solicitor & Jury	4.10
1 Subp.	.15
Shff Wasson	.60
	8.05
1 Capus	1.00
[?]	1.00
Jos Welsh	1.78
Wm Caughran	1.78
1 Subp.	.15
Shff Wasson	.60
1 Subp.	.15
Shff	.30
Fine	5.00
	19.81
Saml Dockery	1.10
Joseph Welsh	1.10
Wm Caughran	1.10
	23.11
D.S. Watts Capias	1.00
	24.11

I assign my Tickets in this case $2.88 cents to R A McLaughlin for value received, Oct 16th 1860
Joseph Welsh.

State of North Carolina } Superior Court of Law
Iredell County } Spring Term 1860

Iredell County
Criminal Actions

The Jurors for the State upon their oath present, that B B Lundy late of the County of Iredell, at and in said County, on the 8th day of April, A.D. 1860, certain articles of property, to wit: One pair of boots unlawfully did sell & deliver to a certain Slave named Hiram, the property of Wm Caughran, the said Slave not having then and there permission in writing from his owner or manager to buy the said articles as aforesaid; contrary to the form of the Statute in such case made and provided, and against the peace and dignity of the State.
Sanders, Solicitor.

State of North Carolina
To the Sheriff of Iredell County - Greeting:
    You are hereby Commanded to take the body of B.B. Lundy if to be found in your County, and him safely keep, so that you have him before the Judge of our Superior Court of Law, at the next Court to be held for the County of Iredell at the Court House in Statesville on the 6th Monday after the 4th Monday in August next, then and there to answer a Charge of the State upon a Bill of Indictment for trading with Slaves. Herein fail not, and have you then and there this Writ.
    Witness, RA McLaughlin, Clerk of our said Court, at office, the 6th Monday after the 4th Monday in Feby 1860 and in the [Blank] year of American Independence.
Issues 18th Ap'l 1860
RA McLaughlin, Clk

    We Acknowledge Our Selves indebted to the State of North Carolina in the Sum of One hundred dollars to be levied on our goods, Chattles, Lands & Tenements, void on Condition that B.B. Lundy Make his personal appearance at the Court House in Statesville on the six Monday after the fourth Monday in August next and not depart the County without leave, given under our hands & Seals this the 25th of August 1860.
W.S. Watts
B B Lundy   (Seal)
H M Torrence   (Seal)

State Vs. B B Lundy, Capias for
Executed Sep the 18 - 1860
W.F. Wasson, Shff

Iredell County Criminal Actions

By W.S. Watts, DS

****

State Vs. Wm. Ballard, Jr.
Criminal Actions
Trading with Slaves
Iredell County, NC [1860]

State of North Carolina } To any lawful Officer
Iredell County   } to execute and return

      On Oath Whereas information hath been given to me, an acting Justice in and for said County by H.P. Helper, Robt. Luckey and John S. Donaldson that on the Night of the 11t^h Instant that the said H.R. Helper, Robt Luckey and John S. Donaldson did see Wm S Ballard receive some Corn from a Slave George, which Slave is now in the possession and employ of J.S. Donaldson.
      You are hereby Commanded to take the body of Wm. S Ballard if to be found in your County and him safely keep so that you have him before some Justice of the Peace in said County to answer the charge and to be further dealt with according as the Law directs, given under My hand and seal this 12th day of June 1860.
J.S. Donalson, JP   (Seal)

I here by Debtise Andrew J Harden to Execute this Warant.
Executed By June 12th 1860, Andrew J Hardin
Judge for Cost and [?] to Court, Cost - $1.00
Ja Donaldson, JP

State of North Carolina } Superior Court of Law
Iredell County   } Fall Term 1860

Robert Luckey In the Suit of, State Versus Ballard
Charges the State in this cause for attendance as a Witness
2 days at 1.00 per day	2.00
Miles to Court & Home, 44 Miles	1.46
Ferriage, this Ticket	.10
	3.56

Iredell County Criminal Actions

Sworn to before me, at Office, the **[Blank]** day of **[Blank]**
R. A. McLaughlin, CSC

State of North Carolina } Superior Court of Law
Iredell County   } Fall Term 1860

H.P. Helper In the Suit of, State Versus Ballard
Charges the State in this cause for attendance as a Witness.
2 days at 1.00 per day   2.00
Miles to Court & home, 44 miles   1.46
Ferriage, this Ticket   .10

Sworn to before me, at Office, the **[Blank]** day of **[Blank]**
RA McLaughlin, CSC

State Vs Wm. Ballard, Jr.
Indictment
Trading with Slaves
J L Donelson, Pros.

Not a true Bill, N D Tomlin, Forman
2 Wit
Pinkney Helper +
Robert Luckey +
Those marked thus +, sworn and sent
RA McLaughlin, Clk

State of North Carolina } Superior Court of Law
Iredell County   } Fall Term 1860

    The Jurors for the State, upon their oath present, that William Ballard late of the County of Iredell, at and in said County, on the 1st day of October, A.D., 1860, certain articles of property, to wit: One Speck[?] unlawfully did buy and receive from a certain Slave, named George, the property of J L Donelson; the said Slave not having then and there a permission in writing from his owner or manager to sell or deliver said articles as aforesaid; contrary to the form of the Statute in such case made and provided, and against the peace and dignity of the State.

Iredell County
Criminal Actions

Sanders, Solicitor.

****

State Vs. Hugh, Frank & Buck, Slaves
Criminal Actions
Burglary
Iredell County, NC [1863]

State Vs. Frank & Buck, (Slaves)
Subp for State
J.H. Dalton, H. Cook & Thos. Brogden
To Iredell Superior Court, Fall Term 1863
Executed, Wm A Meroney, Shff
Come to hand Aug 1863, Wm A. Meroney, Shff

State of North Carolina
To the Sheriff of Davie County - Greeting:
     You are Hereby Commanded to Summon John H. Dalton, H Cook & Thos Brogden personally to be and appear before the Judge of our Superior Court at the next Court to be held for the County of Iredell at the Court-House in Statesville, on the 7th Monday after the 4th Monday inst; then and there to testify, and the truth to say in behalf of the State in a certain matter of controversy before said Court depending, and then and there to be Tried, Wherein the State is Plaintiff, and Frank, Hugh & Buck (Slaves) are Defendants. And this you shall in no wise omit, under the penalty prescribed by Law.
     Witness, H.R. Austin, Clerk of our said Court, at Office, the 4th Monday in August A.D. 1863.
H.R. Austin, CSC
By A.A. Harbin, D.C.

State Vs. Hugh, Frank & Buck
Subpoena for State
George E. Hughey
Executed, Wm. A. Meroney, Shff
Come to hand 15th Sep 1863

State of North Carolina

Iredell County
Criminal Actions

To the Sheriff of Davie County-Greeting:
You are Hereby Commanded to Summon George E. **[Huis - Hull]** personally to be and appear before the Judge of our Superior Court of Law, at the next Court to be held for our said County, at the Court-House in Statesville, on the 7th Monday after the 4th Monday in Augt next; then and there to testify, and the truth to say in behalf of the State of North Carolina in a certain matter of controversy before said Court depending, and then and there to be Tried, wherein the State of N.C. is Plaintiff and Hugh, Frank & Buck, Slaves of Robt. Carson are Defendant. And this you shall in no wise omit, under the penalty prescribed by Law.

Witness, H.R. Austin, Clerk of our said Court, at Office, the 4th Monday in Augt A.D. 1863.
H.R. Austin, CSC

State Vs. Hugh, Buck & Frank
Subp for State, to Fall Term 1863
W.A. Moose, Shff
By H. Cook, JP
Come to hand 8th Octr 1863
Wm A Meroney, Shff

I Authorise and Debutise H Cook to Execute & Return the within Subpoena.
Wm. A Meroney, Shff

State of North Carolina
To the Sheriff of Davie County-Greeting:
You are Hereby Commanded to Summon Geo. C. Davis personally to be and appear before the Judge of our Superior Court of Law, at the next Court to be held for our said County, at the Court-House in Statesville, on the 7th Monday after the 4th Monday in Augt. Inst, then and there to testify, and the truth to say in behalf of the State of N.C., in a certain matter of controversy before said Court depending, and then and there to be Tried, wherein the State of N.C. is Plaintiff, and Hugh, Buck & Frank - Slaves are Defendant. And this you shall in no wise omit, under the penalty prescribed by Law.

Witness, H.R. Austin, Clerk of our said Court, at Office, the 4th Monday in Augt A.D. 1863.
H.R. Austin, CSC

Iredell County
Criminal Actions

State Vs. Hugh, Frank & Buck (Slaves)
Subp for State
Thos. Nicholson & T.C. Cooper
To Iredell Superior Court
To Fall Term 1863
Executed, W.F. Wasson, Shff

State of North Carolina
To the Sheriff of Iredell County-Greeting:
    You are Hereby Commanded to Summon Thomas Nicholson & T.C. Cooper personally to be and appear before the Judge of Superior Court at the next Court to be held for Iredell County, at the Court-House in Statesville on the 7th Monday after the 4th Monday in Augt. Inst; then and there to testify, and the truth to say in behalf of the State in a certain matter of controversy before said Court depending, and then and there to be Tried, wherein the State is Plaintiff, and Hugh, Frank & Buck (Slaves) are Defendants. And this you shall in no wise omit, under the penalty prescribed by Law.
    Witness, H.R. Austin, Clerk of our said Court, at Office, the 4th Monday in Augt., A.D. 1863.
H.R. Austin, CSC
By A.A. Harbin, D.C.

State of North Carolina
To the Sheriff of Iredell County-Greeting:
    You are Hereby Commanded to Summon Amos Gaithers personally to be and appear before the judge of our Superior Court of Law, at the next Court to be held for our said County, at the Court-House in Statesville on the 7th Monday after the 4th Monday in August next; then and there to testify, and the truth to say in behalf of the State in a certain matter of controversy before said Court depending, and then and there to be Tried, wherein the State is Plaintiff and Hugh, Frank & Buck are Defendants. And this you shall in no wise omit, under the penalty prescribed by Law.
    Witness - R.A. McLaughlin, Clerk of our said Court, at Office, the 6th Monday after the 4th Monday in August 1862.
R.A. McLaughlin, CSC

Iredell County
Criminal Actions

State of north Carolina
To the Sheriff of Davie County-Greeting:
You are Hereby Commanded to Summon James McClamroch personally to be and appear before the Judge of our Superior Court of Law, at the next Court to be held for our said County, at the Court-House in Statesville, on the 7th Monday after the 4th Monday in Augt Inst; then and there to testify, and the truth to say in behalf of the State of N.C. in a certain matter of controversy before said Court depending, and then and there to be Tried, wherein the State of N.C. is Plaintiff and Hugh, Buck & Frank (Slaves) are Defendant. And this you shall in no wise omit, under the penalty prescribed by Law.
Witness, H.R. Austin, Clerk of our said Court, at Office, the 4th Monday in Augt A.D. 1863.
H.R. Austin, CSC

State of North Carolina }
Davie County }

A Superior Court of Law begun and held for the County of Davie, at the Court House in Mocksville, on the 4th Monday of August in the year of our Lord One thousand eight hundred and Sixty three before the Honorable John L. Bailey, Judge, William A. Meroney, Sheriff of said County, makes return, that in obedience to the Writ of Venire Facias, heretofore to him directed, he has summoned the following jurors to wit: James N. Cuthrell, Phillip F. Meroney, Samuel O. Tatum, B.W. Parker, Milton Gaither, Daniel S. Sheek, Jesse T. Eaton, William Clouse, James McCulloh, Isham P. Ellis, Pleasant R. Martin, P.H. Cain, Robert F. Johnston, Benjamin H. Eaton, James White, Jr., William N. Howell, Basil Gaither, Mathias Miller, Joseph F. Cuthrell, Thomas Furches, Thomas S. Penry, Jacob Eaton, Caleb S. Kerfeese, Jacob Cornatzer, Jno. Hege, Abel Anderson, Ezra W. Tatum, James C. Thornton, Wilson C. Daniel, George Deadman, Nathaniel A. Peebles, John Brinkle, John H. Hanes, Robert Griffeth, John Bankes, Samuel Smith; and thereupon, by the oath of George Deadman, S.O. Tatum, John Hege, Robert Griffeth, James McCulloh, Jacob Eaton, William Clouse, P.R. Martin, B.W. Parker, Milton Gaither, Thomas Furches, Nathaniel A. Peebles, James C. Thornton, P.H. Cain, John N. Hanes, James White, Jr., Basil Gaither, C.S. Kerfeese good and lawful men of the County aforesaid then and there drawn from the said

Iredell County Criminal Actions

Venire, and then and there empannelled, Sworn, and Charged to inquire for the State, of and concerning all Crimes and offences Committed within the body of the said County, it is presented in manner and form following that is to say: State of North Carolina, Davie County Superior Court of Law; Fall Term A.D. 1863.

And the jurors aforesaid on their oath aforesaid, do further present that said Hugh, a Slave, the property of Robert Carson, and the said Frank, a Slave, the property of Robert Carson, and the said Buck, a Slave the Property of Robert Carson, afterwards, to wit: on the day and year aforesaid about the hour of twelve in the night of the same day, the dwelling house of Haman Critz situate in the said County of Davie, feloniously, and burglariously did break and enter, with intent the goods and Chattles of the said Haman Critz and S.W. Little, in the said dwelling house then being, then in the said dwelling house, feloniously and burglariously to steal, take and carry away against the form of the Statute in such case made and provided, and against the peace and dignity of the State.
Armfield, Sol.
True Bill, P.H. Cain, Foreman was ordered by the Court to be docketed.

State Vs. Hugh, Frank & Buck, Slaves
The Property of Robert Carson

H. Critz & S.W. Little, Pros. Burglary. And the said Hugh, Frank and Buck, Slaves, the property of Robert Carson, were brought to the bar of the Court here, in their proper person, by the said William A. Meroney, Sheriff of Davie County, in whose custody they were. And forthwith it being demanded of them how they will acquit themselves of the premises in the said Indictment above specified and charged upon them, they say that they are not guilty - thereof, and thereof for good and for evil they put themselves upon the Country. And R.F. Armfield, Solicitor who prosecutes for the State on this behalf, does the like. And upon the affidavits of Robert Carson, the owner of the said Slaves, it is ordered by the Court, that said cause be removed to the County of Iredell for Trial.

Haman Critz, S.W. Little, William Blackburn, John C. Booe and H.R. Austin, Clk are bound by recognizance in the sum of $500 each to make their appearance at Statesville on the 7th Monday after the 4th Monday instant to give evidence in behalf of the State. A.E. Cowles acknowledges himself indebted to the State of North Carolina in the sum of

Iredell County
Criminal Actions

$500 to be void upon condition that, John, a Slave, the property of Josiah Cowles, witness in behalf of the State make his appearance at Statesville on the 7th Monday after the 4th Monday instant; Ordered by the Court, that the Sheriff of Davie County deliver Hugh, Frank & Buck, Slaves, the property of Robert Carson to the Sheriff of Iredell County forthwith.

The following is a Bill of Cost in said Cause

Sheriff W.A. Meroney, Judgment upon States Warrant	28.80
Sheriff Meroney, 1 Subp	.30
Sheriff Wasson, 2 Subp	.60
Sheriff Wasson Postage	.10
Wit., H. Critz	1.64
Wit., S.W. Little	1.68
Wit., W.H. Blackburn	3.13
Wit., John C. Booe	1.08
Wit., J.H. Dalton	1.53
Clk, Austin 3 Indictments	1.80
Clk, 3 Subp, 15 each	.45
Clk, 2 Seals, 25 each	.50
Clk, 5 Witness probates	.50
Clk, affidavit	.20
Clk, One order of removal	.30
Clk, 6 recognizances, 2 each	1.20
Clk, Seal & Transcript	2.25
State Tax	1.00
	47.06
Sheriff Meroney for carrying prisoner to Statesville	30.60
	77.66

State of North Carolina }
Davie County }

    J.H.R. Austin, Clerk of the Superior Court of Law of Davie County do hereby certify that the foregoing is a full true and perfect transcript of the record of said Court in an Indictment for Burglary lately pending in our said Court between the State and Hugh, Frank & Buck. In Testimony whereof I hereunto have set my hand and seal of Office at Mocksville Sept 5th 1863.
H.R. Austin, CSC
By A A Harbin, DC

Iredell County
Criminal Actions

****

State Vs. Andrew Kerr
Criminal Actions
Trading with Slaves
Iredell County, NC [1863]

We the grand Jury Presents Andrew Kerr for Trading with a Slave in the year 1863
E.W. Erwin, Witness
Slave of Vandeburg

State of North Carolina
To the Sheriff of Iredell County-Greeting:
        You are Hereby Commanded to Summon E.W. Erwin personally to be and appear before the Judger of Superior Court of Law, at the next Court to be held for our said County, at the Court House in Statesville on the 7th Monday after the 4th Monday in August next; then and there to testify, and the truth to say in behalf of the State in a certain matter of controversy before said Court depending, and then and there to be Tried, wherein the State is Plaintiff and Andrew Kerr is Defendant. And this you shall in no wise omit, under the penalty prescribed by Law.
        Witness - R.A. McLaughlin, Clerk of our said Court, at Office, the 7th Monday after the 4th Monday in August 1863.
R.A. McLaughlin, CSC
Superior Court Subpoena

****

State Vs. M.E. Heyanis
Criminal Actions
Trading with Slaves
Iredell County, NC [1864]

State Vs. M.E. Heyanis
States Warrant
Executed, July 6 - 1864
W.F. Wasson, Shff
By W.T. Watts, DS

Iredell County
Criminal Actions

Nol Pros

State Vs. M.E. Hyanes

J M.M. Fleming, Witness for the State Sworn says on 3rd April 1864 I saw the Deft. Hyanes and a Slave named Sandy belonging to Otho Gillespie go into the Bar Room when Hyanes set out the [?] carten and glasses and the boy poured out a drink of some thing and then the Deft. Gave him a piece of tobacco, when the boy went away I saw no money paid.
K.T. Simonton, JP

State of N.C. }
Iredell County }

    To the Shff or other lawful Officer to Execute and return within thirty days.
    Whereas information has this day been Given me on Oath by M.M. Fleming that M.E. Heganus aforesaid County & State has been guilty of a Misdemeanor in trading with one Sandy, a Slave of the Estate of Otho Gillespie on or about the 3rd April last. In selling & giving said Slave Liquor and Tobacco Against the Statute in such cases - Now these are to Command You to Arrest the said M.E. Heyanis & have him before Me or some other Justice of the Peace in & for said County to be examined and further dealt with according to Law. Herein fail not. Given under my hand & seal this 16th Augt. 1864
R.F. Simonton, JP   (Seal)
Summon for State, Mont Fleming
R.F. Simonton, JP

Augt. 8th 1864. This case coming before me. Judgment & Deft.
For cash	$1.00
Witness	.40
	$1.40

The Deft bound to appear at next Superior Court to answer the Charge on this Warrant in the Sum of two Hundred Dollars.
R.F. Simonton, JP

****

Iredell County Criminal Actions

State Vs. Isaac, a Slave
Criminal Actions
Arson
Iredell County, NC [1864]

State Vs. Isaac, a Slave
Executed, July 18th 1864
W.F. Wasson, Shff
By W A Gurny, DS, 1864

July 18th 1864, Judgt for Cash
$1.60
J.H. S[?], Sol
R.M. Grant, JP

State of N Carolina }
Iredell County }

To any Lawful Officer of said County to Execute and return
  Whereas information hath this day been made to me one of the Acting Justices of the Peace in and for Sd. County on the Oath of Thomas M. Hill that Isaac, a Slave of Dr. A A Lawrence, Late of Sd County on the morning of 17th July 1864 of this & not at the Dwelling of the Sd T.M. Hill in the County aforesaid did Set fire to [Torn] [?] a Barn which is against the Peace & Dignity of the State.
  You are Therefore Commanded to in the name of the State to arrest the body of the said Isaac if to be found in Your County and him have before me or some other Justice of the Peace in and for Said County to Answer the aforesaid Charge and be further Dealt with according to Law. Herein fail not. Given under my hand and seal this 18th day of July 1864.
R.M. Grant, JP (Seal)
Summons for State, Dick, a Slave, TM Hill & RR Hill

To the keeper of the common Jail of Iredell County, This cause this day brought before us for Trial after hearing the evidence it is adjudged that the Deft. Be committed to jail for further investigation. These are thereupon to

Iredell County
Criminal Actions

Command you to receive said Deft into your care until he is Discharged this 18th July 1864.

JH [?]	JP	(Seal)
RM Grant	JP	(Seal)
WF Cowan	JP	(Seal)

Isaac was in the Kitchen which I went to bed. Went to bed about 7 O'clock - his wife and children were in the Kitchen. The boy Answ. - I did not see [?] he came to the fire, the said boy is a son of Isaac & his wife, I understand that Amos lives at George Watts some eight miles from this place, Amos remaineth till Dinner but does not know when he left. The first I heard was a holler and I think the expression was that the barn was afire. The first that I saw was the barn burning when I went to the barn, Isaac was there when I got to the barn, the fire was above the loft, The whole square was burning just not [?] the roof.

The answered Warrant this day returned before us whereupon we proceded to investigate the case of Isaac. TM Hill Called on the part of the State and sworn says that on Saturday night the 16th Just about [?] O'Clock he was waked by the cry of fire & ran to the barn, that the burning of had not been over 15 minutes, that Isaac was at the barn before him, that while up at the fire his dwelling was robbed of an old watch & pr shoes, 1 vest - 4 coats. The vest was in the shade Room. The pants in same place. Coats in same place, shoes in South E Room. The watch in parlor above the fireplace. States that Isaac said during fire he had better send someone to the house as he had heard or known of houses being robbed in such times. That Isaac came from work on the evening before the fire, he had a piece of pine light wood which he split up like [?] pine.

Examined by Deft - Counsel
At the request of his witness he took Louisa, a Slave of Dr. Lawrence with 2 children which he was to keep for her Cloths & bord which girl he has been with him since last January, Which girl is the Wife of the Deft Isaac. I was to take them and see that they behaved themselves & learn them to work - that he needed the services of such a hand & agreed to his terms.

States that Isaac first came to his house some time in March last. Isaac said he came from West Point - Ala. That Dr. Larance had bought him and sent him here, since that time he has been working for the neighborhood and some for myself generally at my house at night. That until Dinner Time on Saturday before the fire Isaac was employed in making a small

Iredell County
Criminal Actions

basket - after dinner he left and went to Henry Hills place, his wife & children were there working out a corn patch. The Basket [?] of was made for my daughter for a school basket - had made several baskets, he and his wife came home about sunset. Isaac bringing the light wood & [?] as aforesaid, I told him I would stay & get out the watch & some other things some clothing, This talk took place the next night after I came back, no more said about it until Saturday evening, told me to get ready & go off like I was going away and then come back and lye down close by. I [?] and said I was going away & went on out of the Gate. I crossed the fence into the sugar cane patch, came up the fence and lay down, I lay there some 25 or 30 minutes, then the fire was started. Isaac took a small coal of fire between two pieces of pine, came out of the door, went round the kitchen in the direction of the barn. States that in the barn there was a wool Cording machine about 1500 feet of weather board, plank, molasses & Straw and a quantity of shucks, bridles, some unthreshed wheat, also som unthrashed Rye. When I got to the fire Isaac was in the act of Turning out the horses at the other barn. Isaac had nothing on but his shirt when I first saw him, he went upon the barn roof of the other barn for the purpose of trying to prevent it from taking fire. While Isaac was on the barn he said that some body ought to go to the house as he had seen the like before & Robbing had been done, he said this about one half hour after the fire was Discovered, the heat of the fire was over when he said this. The roof of the barn had fell in before he said so and the shed was on fire which was also floored. The boy Dick had been here off and on since Spring, was here four days before the fire. Dick was here on last Saturday the 16th Just up to supper. I did not see him afterward. I kept Oats & grain in the barn that was burnt, also horses, Cows, Flask.

Witness Dick sworn & charged states that Isaac talked to me - the first time he wanted to what arrangements he could make to get that watch out of the house - I told him I did not exactly know what arrangements I could make to get the watch then - When I came back here the last time which was last Tuesday he said had made arrangements, he recond would be a good plan - he said it would be a good plan for one of us to take some fire up to the Barn and set something on fire - asked me if I would not do it - I told him I would not - he asked me if he would do it would I stay down here & get the Watch and some other things - In about 20 minutes after he went round up there the fire seemed to be started pretty good - Isaac raised the alarm the family all ran out of the house to the fire - after they all got out of the house I went into the house - took the watch - Went into the Shad room

Iredell County
Criminal Actions

and took four coats, two pair pants & vest - Came into the fron room & took 1 pr shoes - Got the watch in the hall hanging up beside the clock - got the vest out of a [?] I took them off and [?] up in our [?] of the coats and went out - carried them out [?] corn field - left them there & went on to my Master - got there about breakfast time. I put on the vest & coat & I had the watch & went on to Edwin Halls and between 3 & 4 O'Clock they came after me - They Tied me and brought me up here - Come by Mr. [?] & got the clothes and came up to Mr Hills, They took the Watch and Clothes all from me - In the first talk about it I said that they would blame it on the deserter - I told him I was afraid - he said there was many Deserters going about doing [?] that they would not blame it on any of us - Our agreement was that we were to meet on Sunday evening somewhere about Trinity Church. I was to tell him have the Watch and some of the clothes and he was to give me some silver and some pld Bank money, last Friday or Saturday Isaac told me that he was going away Monday or Tuesday to the army to his Masters - told me if there was any danger of me getting into difficulties he would find a way for me to get off out of Danger - I said I did not want to go away if did not get into difficulties - They might find it out on me - I heard Isaac tell Elias Sunday night to tell Amos to come up here he had some things for him.
Ex by Deft. - Counsel
Day that it was agreed that they would take the watch and some clothes. I had been in the house and seen the clothes - I saw them on Saturday at Dinner time.
Of this Witness Testimony
: That he had a talk with Isaac on Wednesday night on Thursday & Friday & Saturday night.

MW Hill Sworn States that Wm H Watts Sworn States that he saw the deft at his Kitchen on Wednesday or Thursday night.

Amos - Sworn & Charged
States that Isaac is his father - That he was here on Saturday night last - That it was about 9 or 10 O'Clock supposes the whole family were not all gone to bed [?] living at George Watts - no one in the kitchen when I came but my father, Mother & two little boys. Father was sleeping, Mother was patching. Was up over half hour before I went to bed - Slept up stairs - I went to bed first - had been sleeping, waked up & saw the light - Called out whats that - looked down stairs saw father open a window & jump out -

Iredell County
Criminal Actions

heard him hollow - Went up to the fire - Mother was going out, came back & got her frock - never saw Dick during that night.
Louisa Sworn & charged.

State of North Carolina
To the Sheriff of Iredell County - Greeting:
    You are Hereby Commanded to Summon [?] personally to be and appear before the Judge of our Superior Court of Law, at the next Court to be held for our said County, at the Court House in Statesville on the 7th Monday after the last Monday in August next; Then and there to testify, and the truth to say in behalf of Negro Slave Isaac in a certain matter of controversy before said Court depending, and then and there to be Tried, wherein the State is Plaintiff and Isaac is Defendant. And this you shall in no wise omit, under the penalty prescribed by Law.
    Witness - RA McLaughlin, Clerk of our said Court, at Office 7th Monday after the Last Monday in August 1864.
    R.A. McLaughlin, CSC

Statesville Oct 21st 1864
By A.A. Lawrence

To Jas. H. McLaughlin, DC	
To 96 days jail fees for boy Isaac 3.00=	288.00
To key fees during the time he was in jail	12.50
	301.50

Dr. A.A. Lawrence	
To Jas. H. McLaughlin, DC	
To 96 days in jail fees for boy Isaac 3.00=	288.00
To key fees	13.80
	312.90

****

State Vs. Dick, a Slave
Criminal Actions
Burglary
Iredell County, NC [1864]

Iredell County
Criminal Actions

State Vs Dick, a Slave
Burglary
+ Thomas M Hill, +William Gurney, + N.C. Kerr, + John White, + Morman Gibson
Sworn & Sent
RA McLaughlin, CSC
A True Bill, J.S. Allison, FM.

State of North Carolina   } Superior Court of Law
Iredell County   } Fall Term A.D. 1864

       The Jurors for the State sworn their oath present that Dick a Slave the property of Agness Rebecca Hampton late of the County of Iredell and State of North Carolina on the sixteenth day of July in the year of our Lord one thousand eight hundred and sixty four about the hour of eleven O'Clock on the night of the same day with force and arms in the County aforesaid the dwelling house of one Thomas M. Hill then situate feloniously and burglariously did break and enter with intent the goods and Chattels of the said Thomas M. Hill in the said dwelling house then and there being then and there Feloniously and Burglariously to steal and take and carry away and then and there in the said dwelling house two dress coats of the value of five dollars, one waisthead of the value of one dollar, one gold Watch of the value of fifty dollars of the goods and Chattels of the said Thomas M Hill in the said dwelling house then & there being found, then and there feloniously and burglariously did take and carry away against the peace and dignity of the State.
R.F. Armfield, Solr.

State of North Carolina
To the Sheriff of Iredell County - Greeting:
       You are hereby Commanded to Summon H.C. Eccles, William A. Gurney & Thomas M. Hill personally to be and appear before the Judge of our Superior Court of Law, at the next Court to be held for our said County, at the Court-House in Statesville on the 7th Monday after the last Monday in August next; then and there to testify, and the truth to say in behalf of Dick, a Slave of Agnes R. Hampton in a certain matter of controversy before said Court depending, and then and there to be Tried, wherein the State is Plaintiff and Dick, a Slave is Defendant. And this you shall in no wise omit, under the penalty prescribed by law.

Iredell County Criminal Actions

Witness - RA McLaughlin, Clerk of our said Court, at Office, the 7th Monday after the 4th Monday in February 1864.
R.A. McLaughlin, CSC

State Vs Dick, a Slave
Subp
Executed, WF Wasson, Shff
By Wm A Gurney, DS

State of North Carolina
To the Sheriff of Iredell County - Greeting:
    You are Hereby Commanded to Summon J. Henry Hill, N.C. Kerr personally to be and appear before the Judge of our Superior Court of Law, at the next Court to be held for our said County, at the Court-House in Statesville on the 7th Monday after the Last Monday in August next; then and there to testify, and the truth to say in behalf of Dick, a Slave of Agnes R. Hampton in a certain matter of controversy before said Court depending, and then and there to be Tried, wherein the State is Plaintiff and Dick, a Slave is Defendant. And this you shall in no wise omit.
    Witness - RA McLaughlin, Clerk of our said Court, at Office, the 7th Monday after the 4th Monday in February 1864.
R.A. McLaughlin, CSC

State Vs Isaac & Dick

Wm A Gurney to Bring prisoners to jail 12 miles ea	4.80
J.N. White & also Moore Grant 12 miles ea	2.40
	7.20

1. Jacob Leruly, 2. M.A. White. 3.[?] Vanderburg, 4. J.W. A. Kerr, 5. John Holdhouser, 6. 27[?]

State Vs. Dick, a Slave
Executed, July 18th 1864
W.F. Wasson, Shff
By Wm A Gurney, DS

Iredell County
Criminal Actions

July 18th 1864 Judgt for Officers Cost   1.20
J.H. Scroggs, JP
R.M. Grant, JP

To the keepers of the Common Jail of Iredell Co.
    Whereas the above Warrant this day returned before us for trial upon evidence & confession of the Deft. - it adjudged that there is a strong suspicion of his guilt - These are therefore to command to be received into your custody the said Deft. And safely confine him in your jail until discharged according to law. Given under our hands and seals this the 18th July 1864

J.H. Scroggs,   JP   (Seal)
R.M. Grant,   JP   (Seal)
W.F. Cowan,   JP   (Seal)

State of N Carolina
Iredell County
    To any lawful officers to Execute and Return. Whereas Information hath this Day been made to me one of the acting Justices of the Peace in and for said County on the oaths of Thomas M Hill that Dick, a Slave of J.W. Hampton, late of the County on the morning of the 17th Inst at the dwelling of the said TM Hill in the County aforesaid, Did set fire to and burn his Barn & Stables which is against the peace and dignity of the State.
    You are therefore hereby commanded in the name of the State to Arrest the Body of the said Dick, and notify J.W. Hampton if to be found in your County, and him safely keep so you have him before me or some other Justice of the Peace in and for said County to answer the aforesaid Charges and be further dealt with According to law, Herein fail not - Given under my hand and seal this 18th day of July 1864.
R.M. Grant,   JP   (Seal)
Summons for State, J.W. White

               State Vs Dick, a Slave
                    Arson

+Thomas M. Hill, +William Gurney, +N.C. Kerr, +John White, Morman Edsen, 1864, Sworn & sent.

Iredell County
Criminal Actions

RA McLaughlin, CSC
A True Bill
J.S. Allison, FM

State of North Carolina } Superior Court of Law
Iredell County } Fall Term AD 1864

      The Jurors for the State upon their oath present that Dick, a Slave the property of Agnes Rebecca Hampton both of the County of Iredell and State of North Carolina not having the fear of God before his eyes but being moved & seduced by the instigation of the Devil on the sixteenth day of July in the year of our Lord one thousand eight hundred and sixty four with Force and Arms in the County aforesaid a certain barn then and there having grain and corn in the same property of one Thomas M. Hill there situate feloniuosly, wilfully and Maliciously did set fire to and the said barn then and there containing corn and grain as aforesaid by such forcing as aforesaid did feloniously, wilfully and Maliciously burn and consume Contrary to the form of the Statute in such cases made and provided and against the peace & dignity of the State.
R.F. Armfield, Sol.

North Carolina } Supr. Court of Law
Iredell County } Dick (a Slave

Indicted for Arson & at Spring Term 1866 A Nol Pros was ordered by Sol.

Bill of Cost	
Indictment	.90
1 Certificate	.30
2 Cont	..90
2 Subp	.45
Judgment & Bill	1.65
Shff Wasson	1.00
D.S. Gurney	.60
Transcript & Seal	3.15
	8.95
N.C. Kerr	2.32
Thos M. Hill	2.90
M.W. Hill	2.86

Iredell County
Criminal Actions

Certificate	17.03 .60 17.63

Witness, CS Summers, Clk

North Carolina }Supr Court of Law
Iredell County }Dick (a Slave)

Was Indicted for Burglary & at Spring Term 1863 a Nol Pros was entered by order of the Sol.

Bill of Cost

Indictment	.90
1 Certificate	.30
3 Cert	.90
Judgment & Bill	1.65
DS Gurney	1.20
	4.95
CM Edsen	2.70
James Murdoch	1.90
	9.55
Certificate & Seal	.60
	10.15

Witness, CS Summers, Clk

****

State Vs. Ike, a Slave
Criminal Actions
Arson
Iredell County, NC [1864]

State Vs Ike, a Slave
Subp for State
Executed, W.F. Wasson, Shff

State of North Carolina
To the Sheriff of Iredell County - Greeting:

Iredell County
Criminal Actions

You are Hereby Commanded to Summon John White, Milus Hill, Henry Hill & Morman Eidson, personally to be and appear before the Judge of our next Superior Court of Law, at the next Court to be held for our said County, at the Court-House in Statesville Instanter, then and there to testify, and the truth to say in behalf of the State in a certain matter of controversy before said Court depending, and then and there to be Tried, wherein the State is Plaintiff and Ike, a Slave is defendant. And this you shall in no wise omit, under the penalty prescribed by law.

Witness -- R A McLaughlin, Clerk of our said Court, at Office, the 7th Monday after the Last Monday in August 1864.
R.A. McLaughlin, Clk.

State Vs Ike, a Slave
Subp for Deft.
To Iredell Su Co., Fall Term 1864

Executed on all the parties
CS Summers
W.F. Wasson, Shff
By Wm A Gurney, DS

State of North Carolina
To the Sheriff of Iredell County -- Greeting:

You are Hereby Commanded to Summon Martha Hill, Frank Summers, Duffy Grant, Richard Johnson, Hezekiah Millsaps, Sarah Lawrence & Louisa a Slave living at R Johnsons & James Murdock, personally to be and appear before the Judge of our next Superior Court of Law, at the next Court to be held for our said County, at the Court-House in Statesville on the Last Monday after the 4th Monday in August next; then and there to testify, and the truth to say in behalf of Ike, a Slave of Dr. A Lawrence in a certain matter of controversy before said Court depending, and then and there to be Tried, wherein the State of North Carolina is Plaintiff and Sd Ike is Defendant. And this you shall in no wise omit, under the penalty prescribed by Law.

Witness -- R.A. McLaughlin, Clerk of our said Court, at Office, the 7th Monday after the 4th Monday in February 1864.
RA McLaughlin, Clk

Iredell County
Criminal Actions

State Vs Ike, a Slave
Subp for State, Instanter
Executed, W.F. Wasson, Shff
By W A Gurney, DS

State of North Carolina
To the Sheriff of Iredell County -- Greeting:
    You are Hereby Commanded to Summon James Milligan, Thomas Holland & James H McLaughlin & James Murdock personally to be and appear before the Judge of our Superior Court of Law, at the next Court to be held for our said County, at the Court-House in Statesville Instanter; then and there to testify, and the truth to say in behalf of the State in a certain matter of controversy before said Court depending, and then and there to be Tried, wherein the State is Plaintiff and Ike, a Slave is Defendant. And this you shall in no wise omit, under the penalty prescribed by Law.
    Witness -- R.A McLaughlin, Clerk of our said Court, at Office, the 7th Monday after the Last Monday in Aug. 1864.
RA McLaughlin, Clk.

State Vs Ike, a Slave
Subp for Deft
To Iredell Sup Co., Fall Term 1864
Executed, W.F. Wasson, Shff
By Wm A Gurney, DS

BE Holland not to be found
W.F. Wasson, Shff
By W A Gurney, Ds

State of North Carolina
To the Sheriff of Iredell County -- Greeting:
    You are Hereby Commanded to Summon Peggy Hill, John Kerr, Baker Holland, Elias (a Slave of Mr Stinson[?] & Franklin Sharp personally to be and appear before the Judge of our Superior Court of Law, at the Court to be held for our said County, at the Courthouse in Statesville on the 7th Monday after the last Monday in August next; then and there to testify, and the truth to say in behalf of Ike (a Slave of Dr. A. Lawrence) in a certain matter of controversy before said Court depending, and then and

Iredell County
Criminal Actions

there to be Tried, wherein the State of North Carolina is Plaintiff and Ike, Slave of Dr. Lawrence is Defendant. And this you shall in no wise omit, under the penalty prescribed by Law.

   Witness -- RA McLaughlin, Clerk of our said Court, at Office, on the 6th Monday after the 4th Monday in August 1864, and in the **[Blank]** year of our Independence.
RA McLaughlin, Clk

State Vs Ike, a Slave
Arson

+Thomas M. Hill, Henry Hill, N.C. Kerr, William A. Gurney, Milus Hill, + Dick, a Slave, Sworn & sent
RA McLaughlin, CSC
J.S. Allison, FM

State of North Carolina   } Superior Court of Law
Iredell County   } Fall Term A.D. 1864

   The Jurors for the State upon their oath present that Ike a Slave the property of A.A. Lawrence Late of the County of Iredell and State of North Carolina not having the fear of God before his eyes but being moved and seduced by the instigation of the devil on the sixteenth day of July in the year of our Lord one thousand eight hundred and sixty four with force and arms in the County aforesaid a certain barn then and there having grain and corn in the same property of one Thomas M. Hill then situate feloniously, wilfully and Maliciously did set fire to and the said barn then and there Containing Corn and grain as aforesaid by such firing as aforesaid did feloniously, wilfully and maliciously burn and consume contrary to the form of the Statute in such case made and provided and against the peace and dignity of the State.
R.F. Armfield, Sol.

State Vs Ike, a Slave
Burglary

+Thomas M. Hill, William A. Gurney, +N.C. Kerr, +Miles Hill, Dick a Slave+, Morman Eidsen, Sworn & Sent

Iredell County
Criminal Actions

RA McLaughlin
A True Bill
J.S. Allison, FM

State of North Carolina } Superior Court of Law
Iredell County } Fall Term AD 1864

      The Jurors for the State upon their oath present that Ike a Slave the property of A.A. Lawrence, Late of North Carolina on the sixteenth day of July in the year of our Lord one thousand eight hundred and sixty four about the hour of eleven O'Clock on the night of the same day with force and arms in the County aforesaid the dwelling house of Thomas M Hill then situate feloniously and burglariously did break and enter with intent the goods and Chattels of the said Thomas M. Hill in the said Dwelling house then and there being, then and there feloniously and burglariously to steal and take and carry away and then and there in the said dwelling house two dresscoats of value of five dollars, one waistcoat of the value of one dollar, one gold Watch of the value of fifty dollars of the goods and chattles of the said Thomas M. Hill in the said dwelling house then and there being found then and there feloniously and burglariously did steal, take, carry away against the peace and dignity of the State.
R.F. Armfield, Solr.

State Vs S.D. Chipley
Criminal Actions
Assaulting a Slave Girl
Iredell County, NC [1864]

State Vs S.D. Chipley
Capias, Defd't not to be found in this County
W.F. Wasson, Shff

State of North Carolina } Superior Court of Law
Iredell County } Spring Term AD 1864

      The Jurors for the State upon their oath present, that Simps Chipley late of the said County of Iredell, laborer, on the 1st day of March A.D. 1864, with force and arms, in the County aforesaid in and upon one Easter, a Slave of G.F. Holland then and there being, did make an assault,

Iredell County
Criminal Actions

and her the said Easter did then and there beat, wound and ill treat, to the great damage of her the said Easter and against the peace and dignity of the State.
Armfield, Sol.

State Vs Simps Chipley
Present Witness
Ingram Laurence+

Marked & Sworn & Sent
RA McLaughlin, CSC
A True Bill, W.H. [?], For.

State of North Carolina
To the Sheriff of Iredell County -- Greeting:
    You are hereby commanded to take the body of S.D. Chipley if to be found in your County, and him safely keep, so that you have him before the Judge of our Superior Court of Law, at the next Court to be held for the County of Iredell at the Court House in Statesville on the 7th Monday after the 4th Monday in August next, then and there to answer a Charge of the State upon a Bill of Indictment for an assault & Battery. Herein fail not, and have you then and there this writ.
    Witness, RA McLaughlin, Clerk of our said Court, at Office, the 7th Monday after the 4th Monday in February 1864.
Issued May 18th 1864.
RA Mc Laughlin, Clk

State Vs. Simpson Chipley
Subp, 1864
Ingram Lawrence not to be found
W.F. Wasson, Shff

State of North Carolina
To the Sheriff of Iredell County -- Greeting:
    You are Hereby Commanded to Summon Ingram Lawrence personally to be and appear before the Judge of our Superior Court of Law, at the next Court to be held for our said County, at the Court-House in Statesville on the 7th Monday after the 4th Monday in August next; then and

Iredell County
Criminal Actions

there to testify, and the truth to say in behalf of the State in a certain matter of controversy before said Court depending, and then and there to be Tried, wherein the State is Plaintiff and S.D. Chipley is Defendant. And this you shall in no wise omit, under the penalty prescribed by Law.

  Witness - RA McLaughlin, Clerk of our said Court, at Office, the 7th Monday after the 4th Monday in February 1864.
R.A. McLaughlin
Superior Court Subpoena

State of North Carolina
To the Sheriff of Iredell County -- Greeting:
  You are hereby Commanded to take the body of S.D. W. Chipley if to be found in your County, and him safely keep, so that you have him before the Judge of our Superior Court of Law, at the next Court to be held for the County of Iredell at the Court House in Statesville on the 7th Monday after the Last Monday in February next, then and there to answer a charge of the State upon a Bill of Indictment for an assault & Battery. Herein fail not, and have then and there this Writ.
  Witness, RA McLaughlin, Clerk of our said Court, at Office, the Monday after the last Monday in August 1864, and in the **[Blank]** year of American Independence.
Issued Oct 27th 1864
RA McLaughlin, Clk.

     Alias Capias, to Spring 1865
     State Vs S.D.W. Chipley

State of North Carolina   }
Iredell County   }

  We acknowledge ourselves indebted to the State of North Carolina in the sum of one hundred dollars to be levied of our goods & Chattels, Lands & Tenements, but to be void on Conditions that the Bonded Simps Chipley make his personal appearance at the Court House in Statesville on the 7th Monday after the last Mundy in February 1865.
Executed, W.F. Wasson, Shff
S.D. Chipley
C.A. Wooly

Iredell County
Criminal Actions

State Vs Simps Chipley
Subp, 1864
Executed, W.F. Wasson, Shff

We present Simps Chipply for an assault on Easter, Girl, the property of John F Holland.
R Gray[?], Foreman
Witness Ingram Laurence

State of North Carolina
To the Sheriff of Iredell County -- Greeting:
You are hereby Commanded to Summon Ingram Laurance personally to be and appear before the Judge of our Superior Court of Law, at the next Court to be held for our said County, at the Court-House in Statesville on the 7th Monday after the 4th Monday in August next; then and there to testify, and the truth to say in behalf of the State in a certain matter of controversy, before said Court depending, and then and there to be Tried, wherein the State is Plaintiff and Simps Chipley is Defendant. And this you shall in no wise omit, under the penalty prescribed by Law.
Witness -- RA McLaughlin, Clerk of our said Court, at Office, the 7th Monday after the 4th Monday in August 1864.
RA McLaughlin
Superior Court Subpoena

****

State Vs. Andy, a Slave
Criminal Actions
Rape
Iredell County, NC [1866]

North Carolina } Supr. Court of Law
Iredell County }
Indicted for a Rape, & at Spring Term 1866 the Solicitor ordered a Nolli Prosequi.

	Bill of Costs
Indictment	.90
1 Certificate	.30

Iredell County
Criminal Actions

4 Cont.	1.80
3 Capias	4.50
1 Subp	.22
Judgment & Bill	1.65
Shff Wasson	1.40
	10.77
Alfred Sharpe	2.66
Thomas Gaines	2.66
	16.09
Certificate & Seal	.60
	16.69

Witness, CS Summers, Clk

Iredell County
Civil Actions

Chapter Two

Iredell County

Civil Actions

North Carolina State Archives
Iredell County Records
Records of Slaves and Free Persons of Color
C.R.054.928.2

Carleton Vs. Bell
Civil Actions
Iredell County, NC [1856]

State of North Carolina
To the Sheriff of Iredell County -- Greeting:
    You are Hereby Commanded to Summon Isabella Chipley personally to be and appear before the Judge of our Superior Court of Law, at the next Court to be held for our said County, at the Court-House in Statesville the 6th Monday after the 4th Monday in February next; then and there to testify, and the truth to say in behalf of M.L. Carleton in a certain matter of controversy before said Court depending, and then and there to be Tried, wherein M.L. Carleton is Plaintiff and J.F. Bell is Defendant. And this you shall in no wise omit, under the penalty prescribed by Law.

Iredell County
Civil Actions

  Witness, E.B. Stimson, Clerk of our said Court at Office, the 4th Monday after the 4th Monday in August 1856, and in the **[Blank]** year of our Independence.
EB Stimson, Clk

State of North Carolina
To the Sheriff of Iredell County -- Greeting:
  You are Hereby Commanded to Summon Mary Kerr, Hugh Reynolds, John Speck, Silas Freeland, Jane Davidson & Miles F. Freeland personally to be and appear before the Judge of Our Superior Court of Law, at the next Court to be held for our said County, at the Court-House in Statesville on the 6th Monday after the 4th Monday in February; then and there to testify, and the truth to say in behalf of M.L. Carleton in a certain matter of controversy, before said Court depending, and then and there to be Tried, wherein M.L. Carleton is Plaintiff and J.F. Bell is Defendant. And this you shall in no wise omit, under the penalty prescribed by Law.
  Witness, E.B. Stimson, Clerk of our said Court, at Office, the 6 Monday after the 4 Monday in August 1856.

ML Carleton Vs. J.F. Bell
Subp Instanter, to Spring Term 1857
Executed of John Lockie
Only J W Lackie not to be found
C L Summers, Shff

State of North Carolina
To the Sheriff of Iredell County -- Greeting:
  You are hereby Commanded to Summon JW Leckie & (son) John Leckie personally to be and appear before the Judge of our Superior Court of Law, at the next Court to be held for our said County, at the Court-House in Statesville on the 6th Monday after the 4th Monday in Febry next; then and there to testify, and the truth to say in behalf of J.F. Bell in a certain matter of controversy, before said Court depending, and then and there to be Tried, wherein M.L. Carleton is Plaintiff and J.F. Bell is Defendant. And this you shall in no wise omit, under the penalty prescribed by Law.

Iredell County
Civil Actions

Witness, EB Stimson, Clerk of our said Court, at Office, the 6th Monday after the 4th Monday in Febry 1857 and in the 82 year of our Independence.
E B Stimson, Clk

State of North Carolina
To the Sheriff of Iredell County -- Greeting:
    You are hereby Commanded to Summon Jane Brown, Sarah Freeland and H M Campbell personally to be and appear before the Judge of our Superior Court of Law, at the next Court to be held for our said County, at the Court-House in Statesville; then and there to testify, and the truth to say in behalf M.L. Carleton in a certain matter of controversy, before said Court depending, and then and there to be Tried, wherein M L Carleton is Plaintiff and J.F. Bell is Defendant. And this you shall in no wise omit, under the penalty prescribed by Law.
    Witness, E.B. Stimson, Clerk of our said Court at Office, the 6th Monday after the 4th Monday in August 1857, and in the [Blank] year of our Independence.
E.B. Stimson, Clk

        M.L. Carleton Vs J.F. Bell, Senr.
        Subp to Fall Term, 1857
        For Deft., CS Summer, Shff
        Executed by J.H. Leckie, DS

I deputise J.H. Leckie to execute the within Subpoena, Oct 1 1857
C.S Summers, Shff

State of North Carolina
To the Sheriff of Iredell County -- Greeting:
    You are hereby Commanded to Summon John W. Leckie personally to be and appear before the Judge of our Superior Court of Law, at the next Court to be held for our said County, at the Court-House in Statesville on the 6th Monday after the 4th Monday in August next; then and there to testify, and the truth to say in behalf J.F. Bell, Senr., in a certain matter of controversy before said Court depending, and then and there to be Tried, wherein M.L. Carleton is Plaintiff and JF Bell, Senr., is

Iredell County
Civil Actions

Defendant. And this you shall in no wise omit, under the penalty prescribed by Law.
  Witness, E.B. Stimsom, Clerk of our said Court at Office, the 6th Monday after the 4th Monday in Feby 1857, and in the **[Blank]** year of our Independence.
EB Stimson, Clk

State of North Carolina
To the Sheriff of Iredell County -- Greeting:
  You are hereby Commanded to Summon Mary Hall personally to be and appear before the Judge of our Superior Court of Law, at the next Court to be held for our said County, at the Court-House in Statesville instant; then and there to testify and the truth to say in behalf of ML Carleton in a certain matter of controversy before said Court depending, wherein M.L. Carleton is Plaintiff and JF Bell is Defendant. And this you shall in no wise omit, under the penalty prescribed by Law.
  Witness, R.A. McLaughlin, Clerk of our said Court at Office, the 6th Monday after the 4th Monday in August 1857 and in the **[Blank]** year of our Independence.
RA McLaughlin, CSC.

State of North Carolina
To the Coroner of Iredell County -- Greeting:
  You are hereby Commanded to Summon Charles Lummis personally to be and appear before the Judge of our Superior Court of Law, at the next Court to be held for our said County, at the Court-House in Statesville on the 6th Monday after the 4th Monday in August next; then and there to testify, and the truth to say in behalf of ML Carleton in a certain matter of controversy before said Court depending, and then and there to be Tried, wherein M.L. Carlton is Plaintiff and JF Bell is Defendant. And this you shall in no wise omit, under the penalty prescribed by Law.
  Witness, EB Stimson, Clerk of our said Court at Office, the 6th Monday after the 4th Monday in febr 1857.
EB Stimson, Clk

     M.L. Carlton Vs J.F. Bell
     To Fall Term 1856

Iredell County
Civil Actions

Executed, H Troutman, Shff

We acknowledge ourselves indebted to J.F. Bell for two hundred dollars to be void on Condition that M.L. Carlton prosecute, the within Suit with effort or pay to said Bell such Costs as may be accorded against him, August 1856.
EMC Suit
Thos L. Kerr   (Seal)

State of North Carolina
To the Sheriff of Iredell County -- Greeting:
    You are hereby Commanded to Summon J.F. Bell, Sr., if to be found in your County, and him safely keep, so that you have him before the Judge of our Superior Court of Law, at the next Court to be held for the County of Iredell at the Court-House in Statesville on the 6th Monday after the 4th Monday in August instant, then and there to answer M.L. Carlton in a plea of trespass with force and arms to his damage Ten [?] [?] dollars. Herein fail not, and have you then and there this Writ.
    Witness, CS Summers, Clerk of our said Court, at Office, the 6th Monday after the 4th Monday in February A.D. 1864, and in the [Blank] year of our Independence. Issued the 8th day of August 1856.
C.L. Summers, Clk.

State of North Carolina   } Superior Court
Iredell County   } Fall Term 1857

M.L. Carlton Vs J.F. Bell, Sr.
    E.M. Campbell maketh oath that he is the Agent of the Plaintiff in this Case, and he does not believe that the Plff can have a fair & impartial trial in this case for the reason that the defendant is a man of influence and he has a [?] several relations some of whom have great influence in this County, and he further says that he is informed & believes that the defendant & his relations have exerted their influence to prejudice the public mind against the Plff and have so far succeeded in doing so that the Plff Cannot have a fair & impartial trial in this county.
E.M. Campbell
Sworn to before me at Office this 7th Oct. 1857
R.A. McLaughlin, CSC

Iredell County
Civil Actions

The Witness [?] will prove that the defendant told him that he had committed the injury complained of to the plaintiff - and that this difficulty between them originated by his imprudently seducing out two boys who whipt a negro girl of the plaintiff two nights before the transaction which the injury to the Plaintiff was Committed.

The Witness Mrs. Chipley accused the Plaintiff and his [?] and found it broken, and is acquainted with the extent of his suffering - the length of time she has been confined.

This Witness is the [?] necessary in consequence of the death of the physician who attended him.

****

Parks Vs. Smith
Civil Actions
Iredell County, NC [1856]

R.H. Parks Vs H. Smith
To Spring Term 1856
October the 6th 1856, A True Coppy delivered
H. Troutman, Shff
By W.F. Wasson, DS

Mr Hiram Smith, you are informed that on the first day of January next the depositions of R.L. McLoud and Napoleon McLoud will be taken at the Sumter Hotel in the Town of Sumpterville in South Carolina to be read as evidence in the Suit Pending in the Superior Court of Law for Iredell County, wherein I am Plaintiff and you are Defendant - where [?] you can atend & Cross Examine.
October 6th 1856
R.H. Parks, Jr.

Richard H. Parks Vs Hiram Smith
Writ Detinue
To Iredell Su. Co.. Fall Term 1856
Executed, E Staly, Shff
AM

Iredell County
Civil Actions

We acknowledge ourselves indebted to Hiram Smith in the sum of two hundred dollars to be void on Condition that Richard H. Parks prosecutes with [?] his Suit by the within Writ against Sd. Smith & pay all such costs as shall be awarded against Sd. Parks by the Court having Cognizance of the Suit under our hands and seals. Apl. 1856
R.H. Parks   (Seal)
D.C. Parks   (Seal)

State of North Carolina
To the Sheriff of Wilkes County -- Greeting:
    You are hereby Commanded to take the body of Hiram Smith if to be found in your County, and him safely keep, so that you have him before the Judge of our Superior Court of Law, at the next Court to be held for the County of Iredell at the Court House in Statesville on the sixth Monday after the 4th Monday in August next, then and there to answer Richard H. Parks of a plea that he render to him, said Parks, two negroes; one a negro man slave of black complexion named Will of the value of one thousand dollars & the other a negro boy named Demps of black complexion of the value of seven hundred dollars which he unjustly detained to Plaintiff damages five hundred dollars. Herein fail not, and have you then and there this Writ.
    Witness, CL Summers, Clerk of our said Court, at Office, the 6th Monday after the 4th Monday in [?] A.D. 1856, and in the **[Blank]** year of our Independence. Issued the 16th day of Apl. 1856.
C.L. Summers, Clk

    Know all Men by these Presents, That We, Hiram Smith, James Callaway, JB Gordon, L.B. Carmichael & all of the County aforesaid, are held and firmly bound unto Esly Staly, Sheriff of the County aforesaid, in the just and full sum of thirty four hundred dollars current money of the State aforesaid, to be paid unto the said Esly Staly and his Heirs, Executors, Administrators or Assigns. For the true performance whereof, we bind Ourselves, our Heirs, Administrators Executors or Assigns, jointly and severally, firmly by these Presents. Sealed with our Seals, and dated this 17th day of April A.D. 1856.

    The Condition of the above Obligation is such, That if the above bounden Hiram Smith does well and truly make his personal appearance at

Iredell County
Civil Actions

the next Superior Court to be holden for the County of Iredell on the 6th Monday after the 4th Monday in August next, then and there to answer unto Richard H Parks of a plea that he render to him said Parks two negro Man slaves, one a negro of black complexion named Will of the value of one thousand dollars and one other negro boy named Demps of black complexion of the value of seven hundred dollars which he unjustly detains to Plaintiff damage five hundred dollars, and then and there to stand to and abide by the Judgment of said Court, and not depart the said Court without leave; and if the said Hiram Smith, James Callaway, JB Gordon and LB Carmichael shall then and there discharge themselves as special bail for the said Hiram Smith, then the above obligation to be void; Otherwise to remain in full force and virtue.

Signed, Sealed, and Delivered in the presence of; R.F. Hackett

Hiram Smith (Seal)
James Callaway (Seal)
J.B. Gordon (Seal)
L.B. Carmichael (Seal)

I, E. Steel, Sheriff of the County of Wilkes do hereby sign over the above obligation and condition to Richard H Parks, Plaintiff therein named, his Executors and Administrators, to sue for and recover agreeably to an Act of Assembly in such case made and provided.

Given under my hand and seal, this the 17th day of April A.D. 1856
E Staly, Shff.

****

Kelly Vs. Johnson & Carmichael
Civil Actions
Iredell County, NC [1859]

State of North Carolina }
Davie County }

We, The Subscribers, do jointly and severally bind Ourselves, our Heirs, Executors and Administrators, in the sum of one hundred dollars, to be paid to A B Carmichael & Stephen Johnson, his Heirs, Executors, Administrators or Assigns.

Iredell County
Civil Actions

The above Obligation to be void on Condition that J.A. Kelley do prosecute a certain suit brought in the Superior Court for the County aforesaid, where the said JA Kelly is Plaintiff, against A.B. Carmichael & Stephen Johnson, Defendants, and in case of failure, shall pay the said A B Carmichael & Stephen Johnson such costs and damages as may be awarded against the said J A Kelley by the Court having cognizance thereof.

Witness our hands and seals, the 7th day of June A.D. 1859.
J.A. Kelly & S. T. Johnston

State of North Carolina

To James Pleasants Commissioner of Deeds &c for the State of North Carolina in and for the State of Virginia, Esquire Greeting:

Know Ye, that we in confidence of your prudence and fidelity, have appointed, and by these presents do give unto you full power and authority, in pursuance of an order of our Superior Court of Law, made in a cause wherein James A Kelly is Plaintiff against AB Carmichael & Stephen Johnson, Defendants, at such time and place as you shall think fit, to take, upon oath, the depositions of Robert H. Davis, O.A. Crenshaw, and Wm. W. Parker & others touching and concerning what they may know in and about the said controversy: And that you take such deposition in writing, and return the same closed up, under your hands and seals, to our said Court to be held for the County of Davie on the 4th Monday after the 4th Monday in February next, together with this Writ.

Witness H.R. Austin, Clerk of our said Court, at Office, the 4th Monday after the 4th Monday in August A.D. 1859 and in the 84th Year of our Independence.

H.R. Austin, CSC

The Commonwealth of Virginia

To the Sheriff of the City of Richmond, Greeting:

We command you that you Summon Dr. O.A. Crenshaw, Dr. Wm W. Parker, Dr. Thomas M. Nixon, Hector Davis, Robert H. Davis, H.N. Templeman, and John N. Cobb, to appear before me James Pleasants, a Commissioner of the State of North Carolina in and for the State of Virginia, at the Store of Hector Davis on Franklin Street in the City of Richmond, on Friday the 16th day of March 1860, at 11 o'clock A.M., to

Iredell County
Civil Actions

testify and the truth to say in behalf of James A. Kelly in a certain matter of controversy now pending in the Superior Court of Law for the County of Davie in the State of North Carolina, wherein the said James A. Kelly is Plaintiff and Stephen Johnson and A.B. Carmichael are Defendants. And this you shall in no wise omit, under the penalty of £100. And have you then and there this Writ.

Witness James Pleasant, Commissioner for the State of North Carolina in & for the State of Virginia aforesaid, at Richmond, Virginia this 15t^h day of March 1860, and in the [Blank] year of the Commonwealth of Virginia.
James Pleasants, Commissioner for the State of North Carolina
Executed on Dr. O.A. Crenshaw, Dr. Wm. W. Parker, Hector Davis & R.H. Davis. Other parties mentioned not found
Jno. W. Wright, DS

This will certify that the negro Man Ben Franklin sent to Bellevue Hospital on the 3rd May last by John Hall agent for James A Kelly was attended by me and died on the 19th same Month - on the 20th I made a post mortem examination assisted by Dr. Parker & Nixson - I found a large Effusion of pus and serum in the cavity of the left pleura, also in the substance of the left lung there was an abcess extending from the junction of the upper and middle lobes, downwards & somewhat inwards for about 4 or 4 ½ inches and sufficiently large to contain fully half a pint of fluid -- His cavity or abcess was filled with pus and lined with a thick well organised pus secreting membrane, with no marks of any recent inflammation of the Lung surrounding the abcess, proving that the abcess must have existed for some considerable length of time & I am of opinion that it has existed more that 3 or 4 months.

O.A. Crenshaw, M.D., one of the Physicians to Bellevue Hospital
Wm. W. Parker, M.D.
We agree with Dr. Crenshaw in the opinion expressed by him in the above Certificate. Bellevue Hospital. Wm.W. Parker, M.D., James Bottom, M.D., Th: Pollard, M.D., attending Physicians of Bellevue Hospital, Thos. Nixson, resd. Physician.
("A") -- This is the paper "A" referred to and annexed to the Depositions of Dr. Crenshaw and Dr. Parker and shown to them.
James Pleasants, Commissioner &C

Iredell County
Civil Actions

J.A. Kelly Vs A.B. Carmichael & S. Johnson
Subpo for Pltff, to Fall term 1860, Iredell
Executed, J. Hillard

State of North Carolina
To the Sheriff of Davie County -- Greeting:
  You are hereby Commanded to Summon Saml. Bailey (BH) personally to be and appear before the Judge of our Superior of Law, at the next Court to be held for our said County, at the Court-House in Statesville on the 6th Monday after the 4th Monday in August next; then and there to testify, and the truth to say in behalf of J A Kelly in a certain matter of controversy before said Court depending, and then and there to be tried, wherein J.A. Kelly is Plaintiff and A.B. Carmichael & S. Johnson are Defendants. And this you shall in no wise omit, under the penalty prescribed by Law.
  Witness, H.R. Austin, Clerk of our said Court, at Office, the 4th Monday after the 4th Monday in Feb 1860
H.R. Austin, CSC.

James A Kelly Vs A.B. Carmichael & Stephen Johnson
Summons, +N.Hainline, +Wm E Booe, +Franklin Hull, +R.F. Johnson
For Wednesday of the terms
Executed, JM Hillard, Shff

State of North Carolina
To the Sheriff of Davie County -- Greeting:
  You are hereby Commanded to Summon Nathan Hainline, R.F. Johnston, Wm. E. Booe & Franklin Hall personally to be and appear before the Judge of our next Superior Court of Law, at the next Court to be held for our said County, at the Court-House in Statesville on the 6th Monday after the 4th Monday in August next - then and there to testify, and the truth to say in behalf of James A. Kelly in a certain matter of controversy in said Court depending, and then and there to be tried, wherein James A Kelly is Plaintiff and Stephen Johnson & A.B. Carmichael are Defendants. And this you shall in no wise Omit, under the penalty prescribed by Law.
  Witness -- R.A. McLaughlin, Clerk of our said Court, at Office the 4th Monday after the 4th Monday in February.
R.A. McLaughlin, CSC

Iredell County
Civil Actions

Mr. J A Kelly, Sir,
    You will please take notice that on Tuesday the second day of October next at the dwelling house of Sarah Whittington in Wilkes County and State of North Carolina we will proceed to take the depositions of Sarah Whittington to be read as evidence in a case now pending in Iredell Superior Cort of Law North Carolina wherein You (JA Kelly) are Plaintiff and Stephen Johnson & A.B. Carmichael are Defendants at which time & place You Can appear & Cross Examine if You see proper so to do.
Aug 21st 1860
Stephen Johnson & AB Carmichael

Copy for Court
A Copy of this notice left at Sarah A. Kelly the Boarding House of James A. Kelly, 25 August 1860
J.M. Hillard, Shff

    James A. Kelly Vs Stephen Johnson & AB Carmichael
    Summons for A.A. Scroggs, Wednesday of Term
    Executed August 8th 1860, RG Tuttle, Shff
    3 cts Postage due Shff
    To Hand August 8th 1860, RG Tuttle, Shff

State of North Carolina
To the Sheriff of Caldwell County -- Greeting:
    You are hereby Commanded to Summon Dr. A.A. Scroggs personally to be and appear before the Judge of our next Superior Court of Law, at the next Court to be held for our said County, at the Court-House in Statesville on the 6th Monday after the 4th Monday in August next -- then and there to testify, and the truth to say in behalf of James A. Kelly in a certain matter of controversy in said Court depending, and then and there to be tried, wherein JA Kelly is Plaintiff and Stephen Johnson & AB Carmichael are Defendants. And this you shall in no wise Omit, under the penalty prescribed by Law.
    Witness -- RA McLaughlin, Clerk of our said Court, at Office, the 6th Monday after the 4th Monday in February 1860.
RA McLaughlin, CSC

Iredell County
Civil Actions

Jas A Kelly Vs Stephen Johnson & AB Carmichael
Subpo for Pltff, to Spring Term 1861
Executed, M.A. Meroney, Shff

State of North Carolina
To the Sheriff of Davie County -- Greeting:
    You are hereby Commanded to Summon R.F. Johnston on Wednesday personally to be and appear before the Judge of our Superior Court of Law, at the next Court to be held for our said County, at the Court-House in Statesville on the 6th Monday after the 4th Monday in February next; then and there to testify, and the truth to say in behalf of Jas. A. Kelly in a certain matter of controversy before said Court depending, and then and there to be tried, wherein Jas A Kelly is Plaintiff and Stephen Johnson & A.B. Carmichael are Defendants. And this you shall in no wise Omit, under the penalty prescribed by Law.
    Witness, H.R. Austin, Clerk of our said Court, at Office, the 4th Monday after the 4th Monday in August 1860.
H.R. Austin, CSC

J.A. Kelly Vs Johnson & Carmichael
Subp for Defts, To Fall Term 1860
Executed, E Staly, Shff

State of North Carolina
To the Sheriff of Wilkes County -- Greeting:
    You are hereby Commanded to Summon S J Jennings, +George Wyatt, +Daniel Hall, +Isaiah Mc Grader, +Franklin Owens, +John L Absher, +John A Absher, +Walter Absher, +John Hall, +Wm. Hall, + Wm. Wilcoxson, BC Gilreath & RF Hackett personally to be and appear before the Judge of our Superior Court of Law, at the next Court to be held for our said County, at the Court-House in Statesville on the 6th Monday after the 4th Monday in August next; then and there to testify, and the truth to say in behalf of Johnson & Carmichael in a certain matter of controversy before said Court depending, and then & there to be tried, wherein JA Kelly is Plaintiff and Stephen Johnson & A.B. Carmichael are Defendants. And this you shall in no wise omit, under the penalty prescribed by Law.

Iredell County
Civil Actions

Witness, RA McLaughlin, Clerk of our said Court, at Office the **[Blank]** Monday after the **[Blank]** Monday in **[Blank]** 1860, and in the 84th Year of our Independence.
R.A. McLaughlin, CSC

JA Kelly Vs Johnson & Carmichael
Subp to Fall Term 1860
To Iredell County Su Co
Executed by E Staly, Shff

State of North Carolina
To the Sheriff of Wilkes County --Greeting:
You are hereby Commanded to Summon Wm. Bryan & Jas. Calloway personally to be and appear before the Judge of our Superior Court of Law, at the next Court to be held for our said County, at the Court-House in Statesville, on the 6th Monday after the 4th Monday in August next; then and there to testify, and the truth to say in behalf of Stephen Johnson & A B Carmichael in a certain matter of controversy before said Court depending, and then and there to be tried, wherein J A Kelly is Plaintiff & AB Carmichael & S. Johnson are Defendants. And this you shall in no wise omit, under the penalty prescribed by Law.
Witness -- R.A. McLaughlin, Clerk of our said Court, at Office, the 6th Monday after the 4th Monday in February 1860, and in the 84th year of our Independence.
R.A. McLaughlin, CSC

James A. Kelly Vs Stephen Johnson & A.B. Carmichael

Summons for +Allen Whittington, +Alexr Whittington, Elizabeth Whittington, +John Hall, +Wm. Hall **[Hull?]**, +Patrick McGreedy to attend Wednesday of the term
Executed, E Staly, Shff

State of North Carolina
To the Sheriff of Wilkes County -- Greeting:
You are hereby Commanded to Summon +Allen Whittington, +Alexander Whittington, Elizabeth Whittington, +John Hall, +William Hall, +Patrick McGreedy personally to be and appear before the Judge of

Iredell County
Civil Actions

our next Superior Court of Law, at the next Court to be held for our said County, at the Court-House in Iredell on the 6th Monday after the 4th Monday in August next; then and there to testify, and the truth to say in behalf of James A. Kelly in a certain matter of controversy in said Court depending, and then and there to be tried, wherein James A Kelly is Plaintiff and Stephen Johnson & AB Carmichael are Defendants. And this you shall in no wise omit, under the penalty prescribed by Law.

    Witness, R.A, McLaughlin, Clerk of our said Court, at Office, the 6th Monday after the 4th Monday in February 1860.
R.A. McLaughlin, CSC

Kelly Vs Johnson & Carmichael
Subp for Defts, To Spring Term 1861
Executed by sending a written notice to Jackson Brown
R.M. Smith Shff, by Wm H Witherspoon, DShff
Come to hand March 29th 1861

State of North Carolina
To the Sheriff of Wilkes County -- Greeting:

    You are hereby Commanded to Summon Jackson Brown personally to be and appear before the Judge of our Superior Court of Law, at the next Court to be held for our said County, at the Court-House in Iredell on the 6th Monday after 4th Monday in Feb next; then and there to testify, and the truth to say in behalf of Johnson & Carmichael in a certain matter of controversy before said Court depending, and then and there to be tried, wherein J A Kelly is Plaintiff & Carmichael & Johnson are Defendants. And this you shall in no wise omit, under the penalty prescribed by Law.

    Witness, R A Mclaughlin, Clerk of our said Court, at Office, the 6th Monday after the 4th Monday in Aug 1860.
R.A. McLaughlin, CSC

State of North Carolina
To Wm. McNeil, Esquire, Justice assigned to keep the Peace in and for the County of Wilkes Greeting:

    Know Ye, That we in confidence of your prudence and fidelity, have appointed, and by these presents do give unto You full power and authority, in pursuance of an order of our Superior Court of Law, made in a

Iredell County
Civil Actions

cause wherein J.A. Kelly is Plaintiff against Stephen Johnson and A.B. Carmichael are Defendants at such time and place as you shall think fit, to take, upon oath, the deposition of Whittington touching and concerning what she may know in and about the said controversy: and that you take such deposition in writing, and return the same closed up, under your hands and seals, to our said Court, to be held for the County of Iredell on the 6th Monday after the 4th Monday in August next, together with this Writ.
        Witness R.A. McLaughlin, Clerk of our said Court, at Office, the 6th Monday after the 4th Monday in Feby A.D. 1860, and in the 84th Year of Independence.
R.A. McLaughlin, CSC

Messrs Stephen Johnson & A.B. Carmichael

You are hereby notified that I shall proceed to take the Depositions of H.N. Templeman, R.A. Davis, Dr. Crenshaw, Dr. Cabell, Dr. Parker, and others at Hecter Davis House in the City of Richmond on the 16th day of March AD 1860, and to Continue from day to day until Concluded and also I shall take the Deposition of John N. Cobb at the Office of Hatcher & McGee on the 14th day of March AD 1860, at which times & places, you can attend & Cross Examine if you see proper.
James A Kelly, by JM Clement, Atto

N.B.
Sheriff will please Execute & return to J.A. Kelly [?] without [?], Mocksville.

Executed by delivery, a copy of the within to Stephen Johnson & AB Carmichael on the 15th day of Feby 1860
E Staly, Shff

State of North Carolina   }
Wilkes County   }

Know all Men by these Presents, That we, A B Carmichael, Stephen Johnson and B.C. Gilreath all of the County aforesaid, are held and firmly bound unto E Staly, Sheriff of the County aforesaid, in the just and full

Iredell County
Civil Actions

sum of thirty six hundred Dollars current money of the State aforesaid, to be paid unto the said E. Staly, his Heirs, Executors, Administrators or Assigns, jointly and severally, firmly by these Presents. Sealed with our seals and dated this 1st day of September, A.D. 1859.

    The Condition of the above Obligation is such, That if the above bounden AB Carmichael and Stephen Johnson do & well and truly make their personal appearance at the next Superior Court to be holden for the County of Davie on the 4th Monday after the 4th Monday in August next, then and there to answer unto James A Kelly of a Plea of Trespass on the Case to his damage Eighteen hundred Dollars, and then and there to stand to and abide by the judgment of said Court, and not depart the said Court without leave; and if the said [Blank] shall then and there discharge themselves as special bail for the said AB Carmichael and Stephen Johnson, then the above obligation to be void -- otherwise to remain in full force and virtue.

Signed, Sealed and Delivered in the Presence of W.W. Carmichael

AB Carmichael	(Seal)
Stephen Johnson	(Seal)
B.C. Gilreath	(Seal)

I, E Staly, Sheriff of the County of Wilkes do hereby sign over the above obligation and condition to J A Kelly, Plaintiff therein named, his Executors and Administrators, to sue for and recover agreeably to an Act of Assembly in such case made and provided.

Given under my hand and seal, this 1st day of Apr A.D. 1859

E Staly, Shff   (Seal)

State of Virginia   }
City of Richmond   } Sct.

    Pursuant to the annexed commission, to me directed, I James Pleasants, a Commissioner of Deeds & for the State of North Carolina in and for the State of Virginia, at the Store of Hector Davis in the City of Richmond Virginia, on the 16th day of March 1860, in the presence of Benjamin H. Nash Esq., Counsel for the Plaintiff and Henry G. Cannon Esq., Counsel for the Defendants, proceeded to take the Depositions of the following witnesses, - to wit Robert H. Davis, O.A. Crenshaw, and Wm. W. Parker - Who after being severally sworn upon the Holy Evangelists to

Iredell County
Civil Actions

depose the truth, the whole truth and nothing but the truth, between the said parties named in the Said Commission, deposed & said as follows:

Present - Benj H. Nash Esq. Counsel for Plff
Henry G. Cannon Esq. Counsel for Defendts.

Robert H. Davis being first called and duly sworn on the Holy Evangelists, deposeth and saith as follows:

1st Question by the Plaintiff
State if James A. Kelly of North Carolina brought a slave by the name of Ben to the auction-house of Hector Davis for sale in the Spring of 1859: If so, state as accurately as you can, the descriptions and personal appearance of said slave Ben.

Answer. He sent one here in the Spring of 1859 to Mr. John Hall; I don't know who brought him. I couldn't describe the negro to save my life. I know that we sold a negro by the name of Benjamin Franklin on the 5th of April 1859 to Mr. H.N. Templeman. The said Templeman returned him, alleging some unsoundness, I don't recollect what Templeman examined him. I saw Templeman testing his lungs, running him up and down steps, examining the beating of his heart.

The defendts by Counsel except to the foregoing answer so far as continuing any allegations of Templeman, on the ground that such evidence is hearsay.

2nd Question by the Plaintiffs Counsel
How long was the negro at this auction-store of Hector Davis before he was sold?
Answer. Two hours & a half, I suppose.

3rd Question by the same.
How long was he in town before he was brought here?
Answer. I think only a day or two; I can't say certainly.

4th Question by the same.
When negroes are brought to this City for sale, are they not sold in a few days after their arrival?

Iredell County
Civil Actions

Answer. That depends upon circumstances. Some negroes may have to remain here two or three months before they are sold; as a general thing, however they are sold pretty soon after getting here.

5th Question by the same.
Describe the color of the said negro Ben?
Answer. I think he was brown-skinned, but I am not certain; I sell so many negroes, it would be impossible for me to recollect the colors or the description of any particular negro.

6th Question by the same.
What became of this negro after he was returned by Templeman?
Answer. He was returned to the possession of Mr. John Hall.

7th Question by the same.
Do you remember any thing about the age of the Negro Ben?
Answer. I Couldn't tell. I would judge him to be about 22 or 23 years of age: I can't say with any accuracy as to his age any more than as to his color.

8th Question by the same.
Please state where you reside and what is your avocation here in the Auction Store of Hector Davis?
Answer. I reside in Richmond, Sir, and I am a partner in the concern of Hector Davis. At the time that negro was sold, I attended to the business of Mr. Davis in his absence but was not a partner. I was then as I am now the Auctioneer of the Concern.

Cross Examined

1st. Question by the Defendts. Counsel.
You have stated that Mr. James A. Kelly sent a slave by the name of Ben to Mr. John Hall in the Spring of 1859; do you state that as a fact within your own knowledge or upon information derived from others?
Answer. I didn't see him leave North Carolina. I only have it from Mr. Hall as being Mr Kelly's boy. He was delivered to us as Mr. Kelly's negro and sold by us as Mr. Kelly's negro.

2nd. Question by the same.

Iredell County
Civil Actions

Am I to understand by your answer to the 1st. Question by the Plaintiff's Counsel that you were present, looking on, during the examination of the negro by Templeman, and that your statement of the Course of that examination is the result of your personal observations, or did you derive any of your information about that examination from Templeman?
Answer. I didn't see the entire examination but saw as much of it as I stated.

3rd. Question by the same.
In April 1859 were you regularly in the employment of Hector Davis, or was your employment Temporary?
Answer. Well I suppose it was only temporary. I had charge of his business during his absence of two months. Mr. Davis was absent at that time.
Further this deponent Saith not
Test. James Pleasants, Commissioner
R.H. Davis

Dr. O.A. Crenshaw being next called, and duly sworn on the Holy Evangelists, deposes and says as follows:

1st. Question by the Plaintiffs Counsel.
Please state what is your profession and where you reside?

Answer. I am a practitioner of medicine and reside in the City of Richmond.

2nd Question by the same.
Please state if you were one of the Attending physicians at the Bellevue Hospital in this City on the third of May 1859?
Answer. I was in active attendance at that time.

3rd Question by the same.
Look at the paper now shown you marked "A" and to be annexed to this deposition as a part thereof; and state whether said paper is in your handwriting and whether the facts therein stated are true.

The defendants by Counsel except to the introduction of the paper marked "A", because it is an ex parte statement and the witness is present and can be interrogated directly as to his recollection upon the subject.

Iredell County
Civil Actions

Answer. Yes, Sir, the whole of the said paper is in my handwriting except the certificates of Dr. Parker, Dr. Bolton, Dr. Nixon & Dr. Pollard. The facts stated therein by me as Medical facts are true. John Hall stated that he brought the negro to the Hospital, as the Agent of James A. Kelly; I do not otherwise know that fact. The Medical facts stated in my certificate are all true.

The defendts. By Counsel except to so much of the foregoing answer as contains the statements of Hall

2nd Question by the Plff's Counsel:
State if John Hall as Agent of James A. Kelly had a slave by the name of Ben in the Bellevue Hospital on the third of May 1859.
Answer. I was so informed. There was a slave named Ben there who was said to be sent to the Hospital by John Hall.

The defendts. By Counsel except to the foregoing question & answers as hearsay

3rd Question by the same.
Who told you that the slave was sent there by Hall?

The defendts. By Counsel excepts to this question as palpably seeking to introduce hearsay testimony: and to answer that may be given thereto.

Answer. Mr. Hall informed me of the fact and so did the resident physician Dr. Nixon.

4th Question by the same.
When did you first see the negro in the hospital; and what disease did he have?
Answer. I saw the negro in the Hospital on the 3rd May 1859, the day on which he came into the Hospital. He was then suffering from a Cough and on examination I found he was suffering from a congestion of one of his lungs; and that he had a Cough which characterised the Whooping Cough; and that there was a good deal of expectorations of mucus from the bronchial tubes. This Congestion of lungs passed off in a measure and the Whooping-Cough seemed in a Couple of weeks very much relieved;

Iredell County
Civil Actions

whereas he was suddenly taken with pleurisy which resulted in effusion in the left lung causing his death.

5th Question by the same.
Did you make a post mortem examination of the negro?
Answer. I Did.

6th Question by the same
State of what disease the negro died and the general appearance exhibited by the post mortem examination.
Answer. The immediate Cause of his death was pleurisy, resulting in effusion in the left lung--or rather in the cavity of the left chest. On his post-mortem examination, I discovered the marks of recent pleurisy all over the left pleura and a very large effusion of pus and serum in the Cavity of the left pleura. On examining the substance of the lung I found an abcess in the left lung about four inches in length, extending from the junction of the upper and middle lobe of the lung downwards and inwards. This abcess on the anterior Surface was ruptured in removing the bony Structure of the chest in consequence of an adhesion of the lung covering this portion of the abcess to the bony structure of the chest. This abcess seemed to be filled with pus, containing about half a pint, and was lined throughout with a well organized pus-secreting membrane. There were no marks of any recent inflammation of the Substance of the lung surrounding the abcess or in its vicinity. That is about all I discovered on the post mortem in the way of disease.

7th Question by the same.
When did this negro Ben die?
Answer. I think on the 19th of May 1859.

8th Question by the same.
When was the post mortem made?
Answer. On the 20th of May.

9th Question by the same.
From the information that you derived in making the post mortem examination, what is your medical opinion as to the duration and existence of the disease of which the said negro died.
Answer. The actual disease of which he died was of very short duration, only a few days.

Iredell County
Civil Actions

10th Question by the same.
From the examination you made after death of said negro, did he have any other disease than that of which he died, and if so what, and what was its probable duration?
Answer. He had this abcess of the lung which I have spoken of, and which, I think, must have existed at least three or four months and probably had existed longer than that.

11th Question by the same.
Could an abcess of the character which you have described exist in the lungs of any one without disabling him and finally terminating his life?
Answer. I don't think it could exist there without rendering any one unsound and endangering his life. I can't say that it would certainly terminate in death, but I think it very probably would.

12th Question by the same.
Was this negro not more liable to diseases of the chest and lungs in consequence of the existence of this abcess?
Answer. Yes; very much more so.

13th Question by the same.
Please state what is pleurisy.
Answer. Inflammation of the membrane that covers the lungs and lines the inside of the chest.

14th Question by the same.
Could a skilled and practised ear detect by anscultation the existence of such an abcess?
Answer. It could detect the fact that there was not the usual sounds which exist in a healthy lung, over the seat of the abcess. I ansculted him at different times while in the hospital and detected the absence of the natural sound in that portion of the lung.

15th Question by the same
Would the Whooping-Cough not endanger the life of one, with such an abcess in his lung?
Answer. I should think it might.

16th Question by the same.

Iredell County
Civil Actions

From the chronic appearance about the abcess, might it not have existed for more that six months previous to death of said negro?
Answer. It might, and probably did.

17th Question by the same.
Would a negro be regarded by you as a Medical Man as Sound, who was afflicted with an abcess in the lungs four & a half inches in extent?
Answer. He would not.

Further this deponent saith not
Teste } O.A. Crenshaw, M.D.
James Pleasants Commissioner }

Dr. Wm. W. Parker being next called and duly sworn on the Holy Evangelists deposes and says as follows:

1st Question by the Plaintiff's Counsel
Please state where you reside and what is your profession?
Answer. I reside in the City of Richmond and my profession is that of a Doctor of Medicine.

2nd Question by the same.
State if you were an attendant physician of the Bellevue Hospital in the City of Richmond during the month of May 1859.
Answer. I was.

3rd Question by the same
State if there was a patient there a negro man by the name of Ben Franklin, the alleged property of James A. Kelly.
Answer. A negro man patient was placed in the Hospital by a Mr. Hall (I don't remember the negro's name), which said negro died and I assisted Dr. Crenshaw in making the post mortem.

4th Question by the same.
Look at the paper handed you marked "A", to which the name of Wm. W. Parker, M.D. is signed, and state if that be your signature, and state if the facts contained in the said paper over said signature are true.

The defendts by counsel except to the foregoing question & any answer that may be given thereto, on the ground that the said paper "A" is an ex

Iredell County
Civil Actions

parte Certificate of the witness heretofore given and that the witness himself is present & should be directly interrogated in relation to his recollection of the facts.

Answer. That is my signature, and the facts stated above my signature are true.

5th Question by the same.
Is the negro patient referred to by you in a previous answer the same person upon whose body you & Dr. Crenshaw made a post mortem examination on the 20th of May "59."
Answer. Yes

6th Question by the same.
Please state fully all the appearances and condition of the patient upon post mortem examination.
Answer. There was the immense effusion in the left pleural cavity, as stated more particularly by Dr. Crenshaw, and also the large cavity in the substance of the left lung mentioned in the said certificate of Dr. crenshaw, perhaps the largest cavity I have ever seen in any human lung. There were no signs of recent inflammation in or about the said cavity. As to the period of its existence, it is impossible to say with absolute certainty. My opinion is that it must have existed for several months.

7th Question by the same.
Please state what was contained in this cavity.
Answer. There was some pus or puralent matter in it.

8th Question by the same.
Was it the same kind of pus or puralent matter existing in abcesses that are found in the lungs of Consumption patients.
Answer. It was.

9th Question by the same.
State, as nearly as you can, what would be the probable length of time such an abcess could have been forming in the lungs of said patient.
Answer. I should not think such an abcess could have been formed under two months, except in some extraordinarily rapid case of Consumption.

10th Question by the same.

Iredell County
Civil Actions

In all your experience as a physician has a case fallen under your observation where an abcess so large and so chronic in its appearance could have been formed in six or eight months?
Answer. I don't think I have ever seen an abcess so large, but as to the period of its existence or the existence of any similar abcess I could not speak with any more definitiveness than in the language employed in answer to the 9th Question.

11th Question by the same.
Is it not a Characteristic of an abcess of that character that they are slow in formation?
Answer. They usually are.

12th Question by the same.
From the appearance of the abcess alluded to in the lungs of the patient, was it of slow or rapid formation.
Answer. It was probably of slow formation.

13th Question by the same.
Are the first abcesses which present themselves in cases of consumption of slow or rapid formation.
Answer. The first abcess is almost always slower in forming than the subsequent abcesses.

14th Question by the same.
Was this patient more liable to other pectoral disease in Consequence of having so large an abcess in his lungs?
Answer. Such a patient was more liable to inflammation and effusion in the lungs, because of preexistence of the abcess.

15th Question by the same.
Would or would not the existence of such an abcess predispose a patient to a Cough.
Answer. It would. It would seem impossible that any such patient would be free from Cough.

16th Question by the same.
Would a skilled & practised ear in anscultation detect such an abcess as you have described by a proper examination.
Answer. Ubdoubtedly.

Iredell County
Civil Actions

Cross Examined

1st Question by the Defendts Counsel.
Did you or Dr. Crenshaw attend on the negro aforesaid while he was ill at Bellevue Hospital?
Answer. Dr. Crenshaw was the attending physician.

2nd Question by the same.
Do you know of you own knowledge and apart from any information you have received from others, that the negro at whose post mortem examination you assisted was carried to Bellevue Hospital or sent there by Mr. Hall.
Answer. I do not.

Re-Examined

1st Question by Plff's Counsel
Do you know Dr. Nixon and where does he live?
Answer. I knew Dr. Nixon, who was resident physician of the Hospital, but he is now not a resident of this State, - I understand. He lives in North Carolina.

Further this deponent saith not.
Teste } Wm W Parker, MD
James Pleasants }
Commissioner }

We agree that the negro spoken of in Davis' examination was sold at Auction for $1260.
Benj H. Nash   p.q.
Henry G. Cannon   p.d.

The Examinations of Robert H. Davis, Dr. O.A. Crenshaw, and Dr. Wm W. Parker taken, sworn to and by them respectively subscribed before me, at the time & place mentioned in the Captr[?]
James Pleasants, Commissioner

Cost of Depositions $12.25
Charged to Plff

Iredell County
Civil Actions

Clerk of Iredell Co.
    You will [?] S. Johnson my atendance in case of Johnson & Carmichael Vs Kelly & this shall be your receipt for sum it is give [?]
April 16/63
S.J. Cambill

Clerk Iredell Sup Court
Sir,
    Please mark my attendance as a witness in the Case of JA Kelly Vs Johnson & Carmichael which was proved at Mocksville to Stephen Johnson as I have sold that ticket to him.
June 14th 1861
I paid him $453
George Wyatt

    JA Kelly Vs Stephen Johnson & AB Carmichael

This Cause now pending in the Superior Court of Law for Iredell County North Carolina

    Pursuant to the annexed Commission to me directed JWS McNeil an acting Justice of the Peace of the County of Wilkes and State of North Carolina at the dwelling House of Sarah Whittington who being first duly sworn upon the Holy Evangelist of Almighty God to depose the truth, the whole truth and nothing but the truth between the parties named in said Commission to wit, The Plaintiff JA Kelly and the Defendants Stephen Johnson and AB Carmichael deposeth as follows to wit. To Sarah Whittington Questions 1st by Plaintiff

Did you know a Negro Boy Slave named Ben owned by Patrick K. McGradey and sold by him to A B Carmichael & Stephen Johnson
Answer. I did

Qn. 2nd how long did you know him
Ans. Four or five years

Qn 3rd what did Mc Grady do with Sd boy

Iredell County
Civil Actions

Ans. He sold him to AB Carmichael & S. Johnson as I have been informed

Qn 4th did you know the boy Ben some four years immediately before he was sold by McGrady
Ans. I did, I saw him every two weeks

Qn, 5th how came you to see him so often
Ans. He had a wife here and he came to see her

Qn 6th how often did you know him to be sick within the four or five years.
Ans. Twice the first time he complained of the headache the second time, I though him of been drunk.

Qn 7th how long was he sick the first time
Ans. He complained part of one day

Qn 8th how long before McGrady sold Sd boy Ben was he sick the last time.
Ans. Some eighteen months

Qn 9th what was the General appearance of the boy as to health
Ans. He always appeared to be Stout hearty and healthy except the two times above mentioned

Qn 10th did you ever know sd boy to have a cough or complain of his breast
Ans. I never did

Qn 11th how long did he generally stay at your house when he came to see his wife.
Ans. He generally came on Saturday evening and stayed untill Monday morning

Qn 12th if had of had a cough would you of known it
Ans. Of course I would for I saw him frequently while here he was often in my house making fires &C

Qn 13th did you ever here him spoken of as an unhealthy Negro

Iredell County
Civil Actions

Ans. I never did

Qn 14th are you able to attend Iredell Superior Court next week distance some forty seven miles
Ans. I am not, I have to keep my bed the most of my time
    Mark
Sarah X Whittington
Sworn to & subscribed before me the day and date above written
J.W.S. McNeil, JP

Mr J.A. Kelly, Sir,
    You will please take notice that on Tuesday the 2nd day of April next at the dwelling house of Sarah Whittington in Wilkes County North Carolina before some Justice of the Peace of said County we shall proceed to take the depositions of Sarah Whittington to be read as evidence in a Case now pending in Iredell Superior Court wherein you are Plaintiff and Stephen Johnson & A B Carmichael are Defts at which time & place You can attend & Cross Examine if you choose so to do.
Feb 20th 1861
Stephen Johnson & AB Carmichael

Come to hand 27th Feby 1861, Mr. Meroney, Shff
Executed by Delivery, A Copy 27th Feby 1861
Mr. A. Meroney, Shff
Postage 6 cts
Copy for Clerks Office

Mr. James Kelly
    On the 4th day of April next at the house of John Barker in Iredell County the deposition of Sarah Whittington will be taken to be read as evidence on the trial of the suit pending in Iredell Superior Court wherein you are Plff and we are Defendants
March 25th 1861
AB Carmichael, S Johnson by Atto

Kelly Vs Carmichael & Johnston, Notice for Depositions
Executed by Delivery, A Copy March 25 1861

Iredell County
Civil Actions

Mr. A. Meroney, Shff

****

Cavin Vs. Long
Civil Actions
Iredell County, NC [1859]

For Plaintiff

North Carolina   } In Equity
Iredell County   } Eliza Cavin Agt JW Long

In pursuance of notice by Plaintiff JWP Caldwell Clerk and Master in Equity proceeded to take the depositions of: **[Blank]** to be made in evidence in behalf of the Plaintiff in above named Suit in Iredell Court of Equity on this the 22nd day of August 1863.
    Jacob Parker being duly sworn for Plaintiff deposeth and says as follows -- Towit

Question. Do you know the boy Jim which Mr. Long, Deft., has now that belonged to Eliza Cavin, if so, what was the boy worth at the time Long got him.
Ans. I was not well acquainted with the boy - but I have seen him. I don't know just when Long got him, he was worth Eight Hundred dollars in Jany 1860 - I was willing to give that without examination - I might have give one thousand if I had examined him.

Quest. What was negro woman Cassy worth at the time Long got her
Ans. In 1859 she was worth 8 or 9 hundred dollars - in 1860 she was worth $1100 - in January 1860 she was worth that.

Cross Examination

Question. Was not Cassy a licentious woman - going where she pleased.
Ans. She was a good deal that way whilst she was with Miss Cavin, she had no one to curtail her

Question. Was not her character that of [?] with negro men & in the habit of running about

Iredell County
Civil Actions

Ans. I don't know that she run about more than any other negro under as little control would have done - I can't say that she ran about a good deal - of my own knowledge the report was Eliza Cavins negroes did run about a good deal - I never heard that she had venereal disease.

Question. Tell how the prices changed from beginning of 1858 up to 1861.
Ans. I don't have negroes rated in 1858, Negroes rate on from 1856 - and [?] 1859.

Quest. What would a woman of her character of the age of 35 years have been worth in the Summer of 1858
Answer. She would have been worth between 6 & 8 hundred dollars or some where about that - I saw Jim at Longs - after he bought him - I saw him when Miss Cavin had him, I never saw him particularly - I priced him from his size & age

Question. What would a boy of 10 years be worth in Jan 1858
Ans. I can not now tell, I don't recollect of any sales that year

Jacob Parker
Assented to - subscribed & Sworn to before Me
W P Caldwell, Clk

A. Clark Wit for Plaintiff introduced - after having been duly sworn - says

Question. What was the boy Jim worth at the time Mr Long bought him
Ans. I don't hardly know I should suppose he was worth then between 6 & 7 hundred dollars - from what I saw of him - I did not examine him any way - Boys of 15 years were then worth in 1858 one thousand dollars.

Quest. What was Cassy worth when Long got her
Ans. She was worth Eight hundred dollars as I could have been sold for that, she had a good appearance, bold, likely, or good looking.

Cross Examined

Question. What was her character as to service
Ans. She took a good many priviledges - run about a good deal - I don't know anything about her work - I don't know she had a bad character for licentiousness, I have heard said such reports, I think in winter 1857 & 58

Iredell County
Civil Actions

there was a fall of negroes - Coming in 1858 - if she had been 20 was worth $1,000.

Question. What would this woman have been worth in 1859 - if she was 35 years old & had quit having Children.
Answer. I have answered heretofore that I thought she was worth 1858 - $800.00

Question. Did Mr Long pay you a debt of Plaintiffs due you - & also one due Huggins & Co -

Ans. There were two debts - one due H.S. Shuford & Co., & one due Joel A Huggins (or J A Huggins & Co.) - Mr Long paid to me these debts - I do not recollect the exact amounts - I think one was $30 odd & one Plf is about that - May be both were $30.00.
A. Clark

Approved, subscribed & sworn to before me W P Caldwell
John Young Wit for Plaintiff after having been duly sworn - says

Question. State what you know about the matters in dispute between these parties.

Answer. In 1st Jan 1860 - I met with Mr Long on the said - I was going to his house to redeem the boy Jim for Plaintiff - I informed Mr Long I was going to his house to redeem the boy Jim, Mr Long said - I've got a bill of sale for him - I said to him that Eliza Cavin did not know that - that she thought it was a lien - Mr Long said that he thought he would take a bill of Sale & give her until November to redeem - I said that there was no redemptions in [?] bill of sale & asked why he did not give a redeemong paper if he [?] her to redeem - Mr Long made no answer - I then asked him how much was in his bill of sale, he said four hundred & Eighty five dollars $485.00 - & then I asked him why he had not sold the negro for his debt - that she (the Plaintiff) would have been five hundred dollars better off if he had, he said he did not think the negro boy was worth one thousand dollars when he got him.

Cross Examined

Iredell County
Civil Actions

Quest. When Long said there is 485.00 in the bill of sale - was it not that he had paid 485.00 of debts for Plaintiffs.
Ans. He said not a word about debts - or paying - but answered as I above said.

Question. When you told Long that Plaintiff did not know she had a bill of sale - did not he reply she did know.
Answer. Mr Long made no such reply - said nothing about her knowing it - he replied as above.
John Young

Evidence for Deft

P.C. Carlton wit for Def after being duly Sworn says

Question. State when as Deputy Shff you were at Miss Eliza Cavins house to collect a debt due E. Bass -
Answer. In the Spring of 1859 as near as can recollect - before the May Court.

Question. What took place
Answer. I got there & talked to her a while - I told I had an execution against her & wanted the money, I would have to have it - she said she did not have the money to pay the execution, I told her I would have to execute some of her property, and asked her if she did not have a negro boy there & told her I would have to take him - she said the boy was not there & did not belong to her & that he could not take him, she said she had sent him off - I think she said [?] - Whilst we were talking Def came in and Plff & Def went out into a room together - she soon returned & said Mr Long would settle the debt - I think after that I am not certain - but I think she said the negro boy belonged to Mr Long, that she had sold him to him - Mr Long & myself came off together, and he paid me off the debt & I gave him a receipt - After we started off and got a short distance - a negro boy, a young boy came up out of the woods & got in a buggy with Long & started towards Longs house.

Cross Examined

Question. Did you not go by Mr Long - & did he say he was going

Iredell County
Civil Actions

Ans. I went by Mr Longs on my way to Cavins - Long said he would be there - I did not know what took place in the room

Question. When the boy came out of the woods did Mr Long make any explanations why the negro was there
Ans. I don't remember that he did - we came on together a part of the way & I came home - Mr Long did not tell me when he bought the negro.
P.C. Carlton

North Carolina } In Equity
Iredell County } Oct 16th 1862

  JWP Caldwell, Clerk and Master in Equity do hereby certify that in this the 16th day of October 1862 at my Office in Statesville, proceeded to take the depositions of Joseph West and William H. Long to be read in behalf of the Defendant in a certain Suit now pending in the Court of Equity for Iredell County wherein Eliza Cavin is Plaintiff and John W Long is Defendant
Present before me - the Plaintiff and the Defendant.

William H. Long introduced by the Defendant after being duly sworn deposeth and saith as follows - to wit

Question by Def. Do you know any thing of the purchase made by the defendant John W. Long from the Plaintiff Eliza Cavin and her sisters - of a negro woman - if you do state what you knew of the terms of the purchase - of the time of the purchase - the mode of its payment and what was the negro womans name.
Answer. He bought this girl Cassey from Miss Cavin - I know this from the Plaintiff and her sister - and Defendant in her presence said what he was to give - he was to pay about five hundred dollars - he was to pay it by settling debts of hers going to other people - the purchase took place in the summer of 1858 May or in August - I think it was in August - the name of the negro was Cassey.

Question. 2d. What were the qualities of the said negro woman
Answer. Her qualities for work were very good as far as I heard the [?] to have a master - she would be good to work if she had a Master - she was pretty much free with her mistress, took any liberty in talking to white

Iredell County
Civil Actions

people - I would rather think she was impudent - it was my notion she was - she ran about a good deal - Her reputation was not good - she was very [?] - she was reputed to have had venereal disease - I suppose she was 35 years old - she had some 5 or 6 children before she was sold - has had none since that I know of - I don't believe she has had any since.

Question. What was the value of the negro when she was sold.
Ans. I think she was very well sold at $500.00. I would not have given more myself knowing her as well as I know her.

Quest. Do you know of any settlement about the price of said negro - if you do - State what you know.
Answer. I was present at Miss Cavin's when they made a settlement and he paid up for the girl - He held some papers against her - he had papers of his own and my own - and other papers he had taken up and Def. Lacked some five dollars - 2 or 3 for paying up and I loaned it to him - his debt was some 70 or 80 dollars - my debts was 138 dollars principal - I don't know how much the other debts were - nor what debts they were.

Quest 4. What disposition was made of the papers.
Ans. The papers were delivered up to plaintiff

Question. Was there any calculation or enumeration made of the papers.
Ans. The calculation was made before the settlement - I also looked over to see if the Calculation was correct and I found the calculation had all been made right.

Question. Was this final settlement between them - and were the delivered up and accepted by the Plaintiff as satisfaction of this price of the negro woman Cassy
Ans. It was a final settlement over the girl Cassy - with the money 2 or 3 dollars I loaned him.

Question. When did the settlements you speak take place.
Ans. I think it was in September or October 1858.

Question. Do you know whether Plaintiff still owed Defendant
Answer. She still owed you some other debts.

Cross Examined

Iredell County
Civil Actions

Question. How long did Def. Have Cassey until he sold her & what did he get.
Ans. It was not long - I think he got 650 dollars - I am not positive.

Question. You spoke of the [?] security [?] - how do you know it
Ans. I have seen her passing - after, I do not know that she was on her Mistress business - she had great [?] - more than any negro I knew of.

Question by Plt. On the day of the settlement you speak of did they set down and make a calculation of the papers.
Ans. I looked over the papers and calculations that day at Miss Cavins - the calculations was made that day - we made Calculations there

Quest. Who made the calculations
Ans. John Long made it and I looked over it after he made it

Quest. What did you go there for
Ans. John Terry came by and wanted me to go - as the [?] could not [?] - to see that the settlement was made right.

Quest. Did you when you gave up the papers to Plaintiff - tell her it was in full payment for Cassey
Answer. John Long gave up the papers to her and told her it was in full payment of Cassey.

Quest. Do you know of the Plaintiff or her sister - sending after records for money in pay of Cassy
Ans. I do not
W.A. Long

Joseph West - Wit for Plf
After having been duly sworn deposeth and said as follows.

Question. Do you know any thing of a sale of a negro boy Jim - by the Plaintiff Eliza Cavin to defendant J W Long - if you do - state it
Answer. I by chance was at John Longs - Plaintiff & one of her sisters came to John Terrys and was wanting some money - as she said to left some papers in the hand of some Officer - she stated she wanted John W. Long to take a lien on the boy Jim - Long remarked he would not take a

Iredell County
Civil Actions

lien or mortgage on the negro - for he did not want to have any thing to do with any bodys property but his own - but he would let her have what money she wanted and he would take a bill of sale for Jim - a bona fide bill of sale - subject as he said for redemption - gave her to such a time - he gave her longer time than she asked - I think he gave her till [?] in October - And if she settled up at the expiration of this time - the bill of sale was to be void and she was to take up the bill of sale. This price stipulated for Jim was less than she thought he was worth - but she did not want to sell him to a speculator or trader to take him off & Miss Eliza or her sister spoke of their having sold a negro girl some time before that to some man in the neighborhood and she had been offered 100 dollars more for him by a trader. John Long wanted to close the trade then and Miss Eliza said she did not want to sell him just then, I mean by closing the trade - To make it final without any redemption.

Question. Long did not propose to buy the negro?
Ans. He did - he proposed to make a final & conclusive trade - but she would not agree to do so then.

Quest. Long did not propose to buy the negro?
Ans. He did - he proposed to make a final & conclusive trade - but she would not agree to do so then

Quest. He did not positively refuse a lien or mortgage did he?
Ans. He did

Question. I wish you to state whether there was an understanding between them that an absolute bill of sale was to be made for Jim
Answer. The understanding was that he was to have a bona fide bill of sale - without any lien or mortgage but subject to redemption at this time - agreed upon when if she paid the money the bill of sale was to be void.

Question. How was Def. to pay for the negro
Ans. She asked him if he would pay debts that came against her - that she was pressed - and knew nothing about business - and was looking, then, for the Officer - She asked him if he would pay debts to the amount of the value of the boy Long said he would pay debts for her.

Question. Did you understand how much Long was to give for the boy

Iredell County
Civil Actions

Ans. He was to give four hundred or four hundred and fifty dollars - I don't recollect which

Quest. Was the price agreed upon between them
Ans. It was

Quest. Who wrote the bill of sale
Ans. John Long wrote it

Quest. Was the bill of sale according to the agreement of the parties
Ans. It was - just as they agreed - the bill of sale was written

Quest. Why was it not inserted in the Bill of Sale - that she was to redeem the negro
Ans. I cannot tell - I do not know why it was not put in

Question. Was it the agreement that the Plaintiff was to call on Long for the amount of four hundred dollars - when she pleased
Ans. At any time she pleased

Question. Was the bill of sale read over to her as it now stands written
Answer. Yes it was - she heard it read and assented to it, She made her mark to it and I witnessed it and it was delivered to Defendant

Cross Examined

Question. Did not Plaintiff ask Long for money & offer a lien on her land & other property - And did not Long without saying any thing about one also [?] go into another room and wrote the bill of sale for Jim - an instrument of writing and call Plaintiff into the room - and say he would take a lien on Jim & presented this bill of sale
Answer. After they had agreed he went into another room & wrote the bill of sale - & called her to sign it - she did so and I witnessed it

Question by Plaintiff. Did you not tell someone that John W Long was to take a lien and on Jim that he wrote a bill of sale for him - did you tell Alex Clark
Ans. I never told any person so I never told Alex Clark - the only two men that ever spoke to me about the matter was John Young & Jacob Parker as far as I recollect

Iredell County
Civil Actions

Re Examined by Defendant

Question. What conversation was had between them and agreement - before Long went into the room to write the bill of sale
Ans. She asked him to take a lien on Jim or some other property and he refused to do that - but that he would take a bill of sale for Jim - He told Plaintiff he wanted to buy him - she said she would not sell him now - or yet a while - She agreed she would sign the bill of sale - he went into the room to write the agreement - she was to get the money and give the bill of sale - He agreed to pay what the bill of sale called for - He went into the room after the agreement and wrote the bill of sale

Question. State if the paper writing dated 18th January 1858 and if marked (A.B) is the bill of sale you have spoken of - and did you witness it - did you see the bargain signed
Ans. It is the same paper I have spoken of - she made her mark in my presence and I witnessed it in her presence
Jo. S. West
Witnessed before me
J W Caldwell, Clk

North Carolina }
Iredell County }

   In pursuance of a Commission from the Superior Court of Equity from our said County of Iredell I have on the 24th day of Decr 1863 at the Office of W.P. Caldwell Esqr in Statesville Calld before me Tho. F. Davidson a witness and having sworn him in our form of Law to testify & declare the whole truth and nothing but the truth of what he might know touching the matter in Controversy in a Suit Pending in the Superior Court of Equity of Iredell County wherein Eliza Cavin is Plff and John W. Long is Defendant he deposeth & sayeth

Question by the Plaintiff. Do you know a negro boy Jim claimed to be bought by the defendant from Eliza Cavin, if you do how long have you known him
Ans. I did not patricular know the boy before Mr Long bought him. I had seen him several times. I have known him since he bought him

Iredell County
Civil Actions

Question. What was the value of that boy at the time Long bought him
Ans. He was not worth more than five hundred dollars

Question. When did the Defendant get possession of said boy Jim
Ans. It was in April fifty nine 1959 -

Question. How do you know he got possession of him at that time
Ans. The Depty Sheriff Carleton went to Eliza Cavins saying he was going to buy or [?] boy, and Carleton passed by Longs on his way to Eliza Cavins, Long got her to go with him after Carleton passed to the same place and after Long & I got there Long & Carleton got into a talk in the house - and I was at the buggy out side, Eliza Cavin came to me and said that Carleton was going to [?] on Jim and that Jim did not belong to her but belonged to defendant Long, and she asked me to take the negro Jim in the buggy and take him home, and accordingly I took the negro boy & carried him to Longs house, and so far as I know he has had him ever since
T.F. Davidson
Taken, Sworn to & subscribed before me at the Office of W.P. Caldwell in Statesville the 24th Dec 1863

North Carolina }
Iredell County } Equity

      To the Honorable the Judge of the Court of Equity for the County of Iredell, the Bill of Complaint of Eliza Cavin of Iredell County against John W Long of the same County. Humbly complaining showeth unto your Honor, your Oratrix Eliza, that in the spring of 1858 your Oratrix being the owner in her own right of a negro boy Jim aged about 12 years worth then some eleven or twelve hundred dollars & being the owner with her sister Sarah Cavin of a negro woman Casse worth some six or eight hundred dollars, together with considerable other property, and being somewhat indebted but not to the amount of one third the value of her property, but being in need of the loan of some forty dollars your Oratrix applied to John W Long of Iredell County for a loan of that sum which the said Long promised to lend your Oratrix, but that when your Oratrix went to the house of said Long to get the money promised, the said Long told your Oratrix that he then had by him only thirty dollars, and that that sum was all he could let your Oratrix then have & your Oratrix told him that

Iredell County
Civil Actions

she would take that & that she would give him a lien on her negro boy Jim, who was then at home some four miles from Longs where they then were, that your Oratrix assented to this proposition, that the Defendant Long handed your Oratrix the thirty dollars proposed what your Oratrix supposes to be a lien or mortgage upon the boy Jim to secure the payment of the thirty dollars, which your Oratrix signed by making her mark, she being quite illiterate and unable to read or write that the boy Jim continues in the possession of your Oratrix until the Spring of 1859, about one year after the securing what she supposed to be a lien or mortgage & when one P.C. Carlton a deputy Sheriff of Iredell County came to the house of your Oratrix to collect a debt for about one hundred and thirty five or forty dollars due are Ezekiel Bass & in a few minutes after his arrival the said Long came also, and took off the boy Jim privately & has kept him from that day to this -- your Oratrix would further show unto your Honor, that is the month of July 1855 as your Oratrix can now recollect the said John W Long purchased of your Oratrix & her sister Sarah Cavin at the price of five hundred dollars a negro woman Casse & took from your Oratrix & her said sister a bill of sale therefore, but your Oratrix Expressly charges, that at the time of the purchase of Casse, the said Long did not pay any part of the purchase Money, but under took virtually to discharge the price agreed to be given for Casse by paying certain debts there outstanding against your Oratrix and her said sister Sarah, among which were two notes due W A Long one for $125, the other for 8 dollars both bearing the same debt due Ezekiel Bass for about $136. Also the thirty dollars due him borrowed as aforesaid & a debt due him for $70.60 old debt for Cassie & another some debts due R O Bowman & Sharp & Sharpe in the hands of one JM Brawly a Constable for collection for about $15 - a debt due John Cavin for $10, a debt due Mary Cavin for about $66, a debt due Alexander for about $26. Ans a small debt due Joel H. Huggins for Casse for about $17. This in the hands of said Clark for collection, and perhaps some other small debts, all due from your Oratrix and her said sister Sarah who were the joint owners of the said woman Casse sold to this Defendant Long, that on the 12th day of May 1859, the said Long sent for your Oratrix to come to his house that day that he wished to see her upon business, that your Oratrix received the word in the fore part of the day and after dinner your Oratrix with one Logan Litton went to the house of Long and on their arrival, the said Long asked your Oratrix if she had come to see about a certain debt, then in the hands of a Constable by the name of Hall for collection, being a debt originally made payable to one Absolom Troutman, but then coming to W.P. Caldwell Esq & which debt said Long

Iredell County
Civil Actions

had staid for your Oratrix, that said Long said he wanted to know whether your Oratrix desired him to pay said debt, or whether she wished to settle it herself, that your Oratrix replied that if she could get the money she would rather pay it herself, that the Defendant Long replied that he would let her have the money being some eighty five dollars, which sum he then loaned your Oratrix and remarked that he would hold on to Jim as surety for the payments of the eighty five dollars as well as the thirty dollars as he had paid out nearly the full price of Casse, that Logan Litton then said - Eliza is dissatisfied about Jim, as she has heard that you have said that you have a good bill of sale for Jim, that Long then replied that it was not so that he only held a lien on him, that your Oratrix was then satisfied and consented that Long should still hold Jim as surety for the money then loaned as well as for the thirty dollars that Long then remarked that the way the business was done when the thirty dollars was borrowed he thought she had better give her note for the eighty five dollars which your Oratrix agreed to & gave her note Accordingly and then the said Long told your Oratrix that he had better give up to her the notes & debts he had paid for her & her sister Sarah as the price of Casse & take her receipt therefor to which your Oratrix assented and the said Long then produced certain notes & receipts & debts, which he had paid for your Oratrix and her sister Sarah, as the price of Casse, made a calculation of the amount, handed them over to Logan Litton for your Oratrix and proposed what was then read as and said to be a receipt for those payments for Casse amounting to four hundred dollars or more which your Oratrix signed by making her mark, your Oratrix positively avers that this receipt as read to her said not one word about the boy Jim, that it was given for the debts he, long, had paid on your Oratrix & her sister Sarah as a part of the price of Casse & your Oratrix shows that she has heard it sai: Long now sets up this receipt as full payment of the boy Jim, but your Oratrix expressly charges, that the said receipt was not given either in full or in part payment of Jim, but for the debts paid fo the price of Casse and if said receipt, which was witnessed by Logan Litton contains any expression of being his payment of Jim, your Oratrix avers that it has been inserted since she made her mark to it, or it was miss read to her before she signed it. Your Oratrix would further show unto your Honor that a bill in the case was proposed by her counsel in May 1860 and she was directed that before it was filed to Call upon the defendant Long for a settlement and a tender of what might be due him & also to demand the surrender of the boy Jim, before the bill was filed in the Clerks Office - that your Oratrix made the demand and settlement since that time, and offered to pay him all that might be due him but the

Iredell County
Civil Actions

defendant refused to come to any settlement & claimed the boy Jim as his property and your Oratrix was unable to meet her counsel until this time owing partly to bad health & this is the reason of the dealy in filing this bill - Your Oratrix states that she is advised that the defendant Long is now claiming title to the slave Jim alledging that he has a bill of sale instead of a mortgage & that the receipt given on the 12th May 1859 is in full payment for Jim, all which actings & doings of the said defendant are contrary to Equity & good conscience and tend to this manifest injury and oppression of your Oratrix, In tender consideration whereof and in as much as your Oratrix is [?] in the [?] in this Honorable Court of Equity where alone Matters of this nature are cognizable and relievable ,may it please your Honor to grant unto your Oratrix, the states writ of Subpoena directed to the said defendant commanding him to appear at the next Court of Equity to be held for the County of Iredell & then & there upon his corporal oaths full true and perfect answers make to all and singular the charges & allegations of this your Oratrixes bill of complaint as if they were here again repeated by way of interrogatory & he fastidiously interrogated as to each separate charge & allegation especially that he answer and set forth whether at the time of taking the pretended bill of sale he did not loan your Oratrix the sum of thirty dollars only and whether he did not profess to take a lien or mortgage upon Jim to secure the payment of the thirty dollars and if the conversation as to this loan of thirty dollars did not take place & occur as stated in this bill & whether he did not purchase Casse at the price & at the time mentioned and whether he paid any thing at the time of the purchase and if so - what - whether he gave any note for the price and whether said trade did not take place in the manner & in the terms mentioned in this bill, and whether he did not on the 12th day of May 1859 send word that he desired to see your Oratrix, and whether your Oratrix together with Logan Litton did not on that day come to his house and whether the conversation in relation to Troutman or Caldwell debt did not occur as stated in the bill and whether the receipt then given was not for debts that he had paid towards the price of Casse and whether at the time of purchasing Casse he had not agreed to pay then any debts as in part payment of the price of Casse & whether he did not then loan your Oratrix $85 and whether he did not at first propose to hold a lien on Jim to secure the payments of the eighty five dollars then loaned, and whether Logan Litton did not say that Eliza was dissatisfied about Jim, that she had heard that you had said that you had a good title to him already and whether you did not deny, that you [?] said so, I admit that you only held him up to that time as security for the payment of the thirty dollars & that

Iredell County
Civil Actions

he answered particularly all the other statements of the bill & that your Honor will order an account of the services of Jim since he has had possession of him and that your Honor will decree that defendant only holds the boy Jim as security for the money loaned & that your Honor will also decree & direct that he deliver up the boy Jim to your Oratrix by paying what may be found due, should anything be found due which the defendant does not admit, as his services have paid all that was due, and that your Honor will all such & other & further relief & make all such & other & further decrees as the case may require, your Oratrix will ever pray
N. Royden, Sol for the Pltff
Eliza Cavin against John W Long
Original Bill filed 5 June 1861
A true copy of the original at Office
W.P. Caldwell, CSC

North Carolina } In Equity
Iredell County } Fall Term 1862

  I John young bind myself to pay to John W Long - the sum of two hundred dollars
  Conditions as follows - whereas Eliza Cavin and Sarah Cavin has filed a Bill in the Court of Equity of Iredell County against John W Long - now if the said Eliza Cavin prosecutes her Suit successfully against said Long - or if she fails so to do, and pays all costs which may be decreed against her then this bond is to be void - otherwise to remain in full force and effect
John Young (seal)
Wit, WP Caldwell

North Carolina } In Equity
Iredell County }

  I John bind myself to pay John W Long the sum of two hundred dollars - conditioned as follows whereas Eliza Cavin has filed a Bill in this Court of Equity of Iredell against John W Long - now if the said Eliza Cavin prosecutes her suit successfully against said Long or if she fails so to do and pays all costs which may be decreed against her there this bond is to be void - otherwise to remain in full force and effect

Iredell County
Civil Actions

C.A. Carlton   (Seal)

Eliza Cavin Agt John W Long
Subpoena
(Return) Executed by delivery to defendant
a copy of Bill & subpoena
WF Wasson, Shff
By WT Watts, DS

To hand the 24 day of Aug 1861
W.F. Wasson, Shff
WT Watts, DS

State of North Carolina
To the Sheriff of Iredell County -- Greeting:

We command you to Summon John W Long to be and appear before the Judge of our Court of Equity for the County aforesaid, at the Court House in Statesville on the 6th Monday after the 4th Monday in August next, to answer concerning those things which shall than and there be objected to him by Eliza Cavin in her Bill of Complaint, exhibited against him, a copy of which said Bill of Complaint accompanies this Writ of Subpoena; and to do further, and receive what our said Court shall have considered in that behalf; and this you may in no wise beglect or omit, under the penalty of One Hundred Pounds. And have you then and there this Writ.

Witness, W P Caldwell, Clerk and Master in our said Court of Equity, the 6th Monday after the 4th Monday in February Anno Domini, 1861, .
Issued the 1st day of July 1861
W.P. Caldwell, Clk

State of North Carolina
To Yancy Dean, Esquire, Justice assigned to keep the Peace in and for the County of Iredell -- Greeting:

Know Ye, That we in confidence of your prudence and fidelity, have appointed, and by these presents do give unto You full power and authority, in pursuance of an order of our Superior Court of Equity, made in a cause wherein Eliza Cavin is Plaintiff against John W. Long, who is

Iredell County
Civil Actions

Defendant at such time and place as you shall think fit, to take, upon oath, the deposition of Theophilus F. Davidson touching and concerning what he may know about the said controversy, and that you take such deposition in writing, and return the same closed up, under your hands and seals, to our said Court, to be held for the County of Iredell on the 7th Monday after the 4th Monday in Feby next, together with this Writ.

Witness W P Caldwell, Clerk of our said Court, at Office, the 6th Monday after the 4th Monday in A.D. 1863
W P Caldwell, CSME

Eliza Cavin Agt J W. Long
Executed Aug - 1963, WF Wasson, Shff
By WT Watts, DS
Executed on John Young & JW Long

State of North Carolina
To the Sheriff of Iredell County -- Greeting:

You are hereby Commanded to Summon Jacob Parker, Alexander Clark and Thomas Lemly personally to be and appear before me, as Commissioner to take depositions, at my Office in Statesville instant next, then and there to testify on Oath, and the Truth to say in behalf of Eliza Cavin to be read in evidence on the trial of a certain suit now pending in our Court of Equity in and for the County of Iredell wherein Eliza Cavin is Plaintiff, and J.W. Long is Defendant, and this you shall in no wise omit under the penalty prescribed by Law And have you then and there this Writ, and make known how you shall have executed the same. Herein fail not.

Witness W P Caldwell, Clerk and Master of our said Court of Equity, on the 7th day of August A.D., 1863.
W P Caldwell, CSME

Cavin Agt Long
Notice for deft, Oct 1862
A Copy of the same delivered Oct 10 - 1862
WF Wasson, Shff
By WT Watts, DS

Iredell County
Civil Actions

The boy Jim remains in possession of Plaintiff until first of April 1859 when the Plff delivers up **[Faded]** to the defendant on account of his right by the Bill of Sale aforesaid

Mrs Eliza Cavin
        Mrs Eliza Cavin
You are Notified that on the 16th October Past and at the Court House in Statesville the deposition of John W Long, Jos. S. Trent[?] & others will be taken to be read as evidence in the suit pending in the Superior Court of Equity for Iredell County wherein you are Plff & I am defendant when & wgere you may stand & Cross Examine.
Oct 9th 1862
J.W. Long

                Cavin Vs Long
Copy of notes for deposition in Equity
                Execited 1863
                WF Wasson, Shff
                T W Watts, DS
        To Hand December 18 1863

Miss Eliza Cavin I will on the 24th Instant at the Office of WP Caldwell Esquire in Statesville take the deposition of T.F. Davidson & others to be offered as evidence in the suit wherein you are Plff & I am Deft pending in Superior Court Of Equity for Iredell County. Decr. 15 1863
JW Long, By Atto

            Eliza Cavin agt J.W. Long
            Subpoena to 16 May 1863
            Executed Apr 21 - 1863
            W.F. Wasson, Shff
            By T W. Watts, DS

State of North Carolina
To the Sheriff of Iredell County -- Greeting:
        You are hereby Commanded to Summon Jacob Parker, Alexander Clark and John Young personall to be and appear before me, as

Iredell County
Civil Actions

Commissioner to take Depositions, at my Office in Statesville on the 16th day of May (Saturday) next, then and there to testify on Oath, and the Truth to say in behalf of Eliza Cavin to be read as evidence on the trial of a certain suit now pending in our Court of Equity in and for the County of Iredell wherein Eliza Cavin is Plaintiff and John W. Long is Defendant, and this you shall in no wise omit under the penalty prescribed by Law. And have then and there this Writ. And make known how you shall have executed the same. Herein fail not.

Witness W P Caldwell, Clerk and Master of our said Court of Equity, on the 1st day of April A.D. 1863.
WP Caldwell, CSC

Cavin Vs JW Long
Subp to May 16th, Executed 1863

May the 14th 1863, by leaving a Written notice at his residence
W.F. Wasson, Shff
Z.W.T. Watts, DS

State of North Carolina
To the Sheriff of Iredell County--Greeting:

You are hereby Commanded to Summon Thomas Lemly personally to be and appear before me, as Commissioner to take Depositions, at My Office in Statesville on the 16th day of May next, then and there to testify on Oath, and the Truth to say in behalf of Sarah Cavin to be read as evidence on the trial of a certain suit now pending in our Court of Equity in and for the County of Iredell wherein sarah Cavin is Plaintiff and J W Long is Defendant, and this you shall in no wise omit under the penalty prescribed by Law. And have you then and there this Writ, and make known how you shall have executed the same. Herein fail not.

Witness, W.P. Caldwell, Clerk and Master of our said Court of Equity, on the 14th day of May A.D. 1863.
WP Caldwell, CSC

North Carolina   } Superior Court in Equity
Iredell County   } Fall Term 1862

Iredell County
Civil Actions

To the Honourable the Judge of the Court of Equity in and for the County of Iredell; The Answer of John Long to the Bill of Complaint of Eliza Cavin against him.

This Defendant answering saith that in the month of January 1858 the Plaintiff applied thru another person to this Defendant to borrow thirty dollars & not to borrow thirty dollars & not to borrow forty dollars as erroneously alleged in her Bill; This Defendant no then having in hand that sum of thirty dollars appointed a certain Subsequent day on which he would be able to loan the sum required & on the day appointed Towit 18th January 1858 this Defendant having procured the sum required for to wit thirty dollars, the Plaintiff applied for it at Defendants own house and then and there received it -- The Plaintiff on this last named day proposed to borrow thirty dollars & no other sum according to the best of the knowledge in his remembrance & belief of this Defendant -- The Plaintiff said she was willing to give a lien on any thing she had as security for the repayment of the money borrowed -- The Defendant replied he did not want any lien or Mortgage and would not take any -- He continued and said she had a negro boy named Jim, he would be glad to purchase -- She affected to be unwilling to Sell -- This Defendant to induce her to sell proposed that if against the coming October she had not become satisfied with the sale, she might then repurchase on repaying to this Defendant the price of the boy or such part of it or up to that time he should have [?] to her -- And if she would agree to on these terms he would give for the boy four hundred dollars; But he expressly distinctly stipulated with her that she should give a perfect and unconditional Bill of Sale for the Conveyance of the boy to this Defendant, reciting the Consideration of four hundred dollars; The Plaintiff understood these terms & stipulations as here alleged and with full knowledge of their import [?] assented to them -- She knew this Defendant wanted no lien or Mortgage & would & would take none -- He proposed a purchase, which she knew he wanted an absolute Bill of Sale, which she also knew & consented to give -- The Bill of Sale was written by this deponent in accordance to this understanding & agreement of the Plff & himself and after was distinctly thereby read over to her & she signed & executed it with a full knowledge of its contents & it was then attended by the Subscribing witnesses --The boy Jim was sold to this Defendant as being ten years of age -- This Defendant did not propose to take lien or Mortgage on the said boy as falsely alleged in Plaintiffs Bill -- The offer of Plff to give a lien on her property was made as herein before admitted -- The Plff retained possession of the sd boy until April 1859

Iredell County
Civil Actions

when this Defendant seeing an Officer P. Carleton pass his house on his way to the house of Plff, as Officer alleged with an Execution against her & hearing him declare his intention to seize or lien on a Negro boy knowing if Plff had another slave he was about from home, this Deft accompanied the Officer to the Plffs house -- And when he arrived at her house the Plff advised the Defendant to take his Negro Jim home for Carleton talked about taking home [?] she immediately surrendered up the said boy to him to carry home as his own property which he according to another person did & has retained possession of him ever since -- It is true that several days previous to the 12th day of May 1859 the Defendant sent word to Plff to come to his house sending her at the same time words that the business he had for her was to deliver to her [?] or notes which he had pd off in paying for Jim -- She came as in her Bill alleged with one Logan Litton to the place of this Defendant and a consultation was had with her as to the payments he had made for & on account of the sd boy Jim & this consultation was had in the presence to said Logan Litton and it was then 3rd ascertained that the payments which this Defendant had made to & for her towards the payment for Sd boy amounted to four hundred eighty five dollars and the Defendant surrendered to the Plff at that time the evidences of the debts which he had paid for her as well as evidences of advancements of money made to herself; These payments & advancements had made her at the instance [?] of Plff. They included among others evidences of advancements to Plff herself of the thirty dollars loaned to her on the date of the Bill of Sale, one hundred & sixty seven dollars & 94 cents advanced to her on the first of May 1858, sixty five dollars paid on a judgment against her of A Troutman or W.P. Caldwell about seventeen dollars paid on a debt of Logan Litton, one Judgment in favour of [?] & about ten dollars to one John Cavin on his debt against her, one against her for about 45.00 & one judgment in hands of Rumple against her for one hundred & thirty six dollars on an execution against her and in favour of one Ezekiel Bass & a debt to A. Logan for five dollars. The Defendant is unable to recite or name each debt with exact amounts, being unable to do so for the reason that he surrendered to the Plff the vouchers for his payments and she **[Line marked through, indecipherable]** There was also other payments made for her behalf of Sd Eliza Cavin in payment of the price of Jim as this Defendant will be able to show.

This Defendant has no recollection or belief that the conversation concerning a debt coming to W.P. Caldwell Esqr stated in Plffs Bill occurred, debt had been paid for the Plff by this Deft to the Constable Hall several months before the 12th of May 1859 was [?] that day [?] to this

Iredell County
Civil Actions

~~Deft as a payment towards the price of Jim~~. The amount of that debt as well as this defendant recollects was sixty five dollars & not eighty five dollars as in Plff Bill is erroniously stated -- This Defendant did not remark or say that he would hold on to Jim as security for the payment of eighty five dollars loaned to Plff as well as the thirty dollars nor did he make any remark of similar import; This Defendant has no recollection or belief that Logan Litton said when that occasion "Eliza is dissatisfied about Jim as she has heard you (Deft) have said you have a good Bill of Sale for Jim" & that this Defendant then said it was not so, and that he only holds a lien on him; This Defendant positively denies the language imparted to him in the the said allegation & to the best of his knowledge & belief the entire alleged Colloquism is false.

    This Defendant further answering says it is true that in the month of August 1858 the Plff with her sisters, Sarah & Mary sold to him a negro woman Slave Cassie; The said Slave had displeased her owners, had left their service & was living away from home, had the reputation of being unruly & very [?] in her communion with men & **[Line marked through, indecipherable]** & was suspected of being [?]. Her owners agreed to sell her to this Defendant for five hundred dollars & he purchased her for that price -- and it was part of the agreement that Defendant should discharge the debt for the [?] paying debts against his Vendors to the amount of the price --The name of the said Slave was Cassy -- The Deft paid to the Plff & one of her sisters within a five days in cash twelve dollars, paid to them or some one of them Bacon to the value of $2.10 Cts. Paid several notes for them they owed to one Alexr Clark about thirty four dollars & fifty four cents -- to the same on a debt owing by some of them to one Joel Huggins for twenty dollars, a debt they or some of them owed Jenkins Taylor of Charlotte for about fifty one dollars, two debts they or some of them owed to one Wm. H. Long for about one hundred & thirty eight dollars, a debt against them or some of them due to Mary Cavin for sixty six dollars principal money, to Solom Clodfelter several debts them or some of them owed for nineteen dollars -- debt to C.A. Carlton against them or some of them about thirty eight dollars -- a debt against some of them to one Ro. Brown about eight dollars & 25 cts pl money & debt to Sharpe & Sharpe against some of them for about thirty dollars & in addition they or some of them owed this Defendant by note Seventy eight dollars sixty cents -- The debts here innumerated as paid for Plff & her sisters were paid at the request of Plff or her sister Sarah & was paid towards the price of the negro woman Cassy & were all paid before the end of Sept 1858 -- and towards the end of September or about the first of October, this Defendant

Iredell County
Civil Actions

came to an accurate settlement with the Plff & her sister Sarah over the payments he had made them & for them on account of the price to be paid for the woman Cassie -- The settlement was made in the presence & assistance of one Wm H Long, And by the account made between us it was ascertained this Defendant was still owing a small sum for negro woman which sum he borrowed from sd Wm H. Long & immediately paid over to Plff or her sister Sarah -- At this time [?] towards the end of Sept or about the first of October 1858 the evidences of the debts to Alex Clark to Joel Huggins, to Wm H Long, the debt for seventy eight dollars & sixty cents, The debts to Mary Cavin, to R.O. Browns, to Sharpe & Sharpe were with the [?] of the other debts above mentioned delivered up to the Plaintiff and were not delivered up to Plaintiff by this Defendant on the 12th of May 1859 at the time she gave her receipt of that date as by Plff in her Bill falsely alleged. This Defendant further answering says it is not true that on the 12th May 1859 this Defendant told the Plff he had better give up to her the notes and debts he had pd for her & her sister Sarah as the price of Cassie & that he produced [?] Logan Litton for the Plff certain notes, receipts & debts he had paid for Plff & her sister Sarah as the price of Cassie as falsely alleged in Plffs Bill; all such notes, receipts & debts had been handed over to the Plff on the settlement concerning the price of Cassie towards the last of Sept. about five [?] Oct 1858 -- It is not true that this Defendant prepared on the 12th day of May 1859 any paper writing purporting to be a receipt for payments of notes & debts for the Plff and her sister Sarah by this Defendant on account of the price of the negro woman Cassie -- It is not true that he prepared on that day any paper writing that was read as and was said to be a receipt for such payments -- It is untrue that the said paper writing was on that day prepared & read to the Plff, said not one word about Jim, but in truth and in fact it was read to her as a receipt in full payment of a four hundred and eighty five dollar & 15/100 dollars in full of cash, notes, & receipts said Long was to settle for me (Eliza Cavin in the purchase of negro boy I sold - him by the name of Jim.) It is not true that receipt was not given either in full or part payment for the price of Jim, but for debts paid for the price of Cassie, but in truth & in fact it was given in full for the payment of the price of Jim & was not given for the payment of the price of Cassie in full or in part -- Said paper writing was passed as a receipt in full to be signed by the Plffs acknowledging payment in full of the price of the boy Jim -- It was read truly as it was written -- no misrepresentations of its meaning was employed & no [?] given of its import -- This Defendant required her to sign a receipt for the payment of Jim & she did so and this Defendant

Iredell County
Civil Actions

believes & doth ask she did so with a correct knowledge of its import -- And it is untrue that any alteration has been made in said receipt by addition thereto or by taking anything therefrom -- or by any change in its words since the Plff signed by making her mark to it.

  This Defendant further answering shows the Plaintiff received from him the [?] of the debts which he had paid for her and of debts which she owed him and without any notice to him she retained any right in or to the boy Jim; All these evidences of debts as far as this [?] Defendant believes remain in her possession & she allowed him to remain unmindful of her purpose, if she [?] it, of prosecuting her unjust claim against him untill it should be when difficult if not impossible to establish by proof of each payment & [?] which he has made to the Plaintiff -- The receipt dated 12th May 1859 & signed by her & attested by Logan Litton was given by her as an express acknowledgement of full payment for the boy Jim after all the receipts of payment had been examined, [?], & calculated by Sd Litton & this Defendant and the result fairly & truly ascertained & made known to her.

  This Defendant further answers says that he is informed & believes & doth Answers that the Plaintiffs Bill was filed in this Suit on the 5th of June 1861 and not before and he relies upon the protection of this Statute Chapter 65, receipt code limiting the time [?] the commencement of dates in the same [?] as if the same was here specially pleaded.

  He has no knowledge or notice of a Bill having been prepared for Plffs in May 1860 except what he has required from the [?] Bill she [?] such was the case having answered he prays the [?].
A. Mitchell for Deft.

  The Defendant John W. Long appeared before me and made oath that the matters of fact stated in his forgoing Answer as of his own knowledge are true and such as are Stated as of matters of belief, he believes to be true.
Subscribed & Sworn to before me
W.P. Caldwell, CSC
Eliza Cavin Vs John W Long
Answer of Deft.
To Fall Term 1862, A.M.

      Eliza Cavin Agt John Long
       Aug 22nd 1863

Iredell County Civil Actions

A Clark, Wit for Plaintiff
Charges 1 day .60
22 .44
1.04
Ticket .10
1.14
W.P. Caldwell

Jacob Parker Charges Pltff
As Wit 1 day .60
14 Ticket .28
Ticket .10
.98
W.P. Caldwell

John Young Charges Pltff .68
Ticket .32
.10
1.02
W P Caldwell

TB Lemly charges Pltff .60
.44
Ticket .10
1.14

****

M. L. Nesbet Vs Jacob Ramsour
Civil Actions
Iredell County, NC [1860]

M L Nesbet Vs Jacob Ramsour

Jacob Parkes agent for the Plaintiff maketh Oath that the Plaintiff cannot come safely to trial for the want of the testimony of Jacob Trollenger and Grafton [?] who are under Subpoena and absent without his consent or procurement - that he expects to prove by said Witnesses that the negro Boy AB warranted in the Bill of Sale to a [?] - was in fact answered Jacob Parkes **[Parker]**

Iredell County
Civil Actions

Sworn to & subscribed
R.A. McLaughlin, CSC

M. L. Nesbit Vs Jacob Ramseur

North Carolina } Superior Court
Iredell County   } Fall Term

M L Nesbit Vs Jacob Ramsour

Jacob Parkes, Agt., for Plaintiff Maketh oath that the Plaintiff cannot come safely to trial for the want of the testimony of Graften Gardner who is under Subpoena and is absent without his consent.
He expects to prove by said Witness that the slave was answered at the time Plaintiff purchased from Defendant.
That said Wit is absent from the State as he is informed, and he expects this benefit of his testimony at the next term of this Court. And that this affidavit is next made for delay.
Jacob Parkes
Sworn to & Subscribed
R.A. McLaughlin, CSC

ML Nesbit Vs Jacob Ramsour

Jacob Parkes agent of Plaintiff maketh oath that he cannot come safely to trial for the want of the testimony of Graften Gardner who is under subpoena and is absent without his consent or procurement.
Plaintiff expects to prove by said witness that the negro slave who was conveyed by Defendant to Plaintiff was answered - that he bought the negro - sent [?] Defendants and took him back to Deft - [?] he was answered that said [?] - as he is informed went to Alabama last fall with a large lot of slaves to sell - but that he has been detained out of the State by [?] of delays in making sales of his slaves.
That he protests the testimony of said witness at the next term of this Court.
Jacob Parkes
Sworn to subscribed

Iredell County
Civil Actions

R.A. McLaughlin

****

Young Vs Mills
Civil Actions
Iredell County, NC [1861]

John Young Vs George Mills
To Fall 1861

To Oct Term 1861 Levied the Execution on 2 Negroes named [?], Henry W.F. Wasson, Shff
By W T Watts, DS

State of North Carolina
To the Sheriff of Iredell County -- Greeting:

We Command You, That of the Goods and Chattles, Lands and Tenements of George Mills & Geo. S. Kerr if to be found in your County you cause to be made the sum of $370. 59 cts of which sum $348.09 is his money with Interest from April 8th 1861 to be paid, which was lately in our Superior Court of Law held for Iredell County, at the Court House in Statesville adjudged John Young for debt, besides the further sum of $18. 80 cents for Costs and Charges in the said suit expended, whereof the said Defendant above named as liable as appears to us of record: And have you the said monies besides your fees for this service, before our said Court at Statesville aforesaid, on the 6th Monday after the 4th Monday in August next, then and there to render the said Debt, Cost and Charges aforesaid. Herein fail not, and have you then and there this Writ.

Witness, RA McLaughlin, Clerk of our said Court at office, the 6th Monday after the 4th Monday in February 1861.
May 10th 1861
RA McLaughlin, CSC

Debt	348.09
Int.	9.45
" at 10 pctl	3.05
	370.59

Iredell County
Civil Actions

Co Co Cost	
Wn't - Tax & bord	2.40
1 Court Indict & Bill	1.40
Appeal Bond	.60
[?]	2.25
Shff Wasson	1.00
Atto W.P.C.	4.00
	11.65
Superior Costs	
Entering appeal	1.00
Indict & Bill	1.00
Appeal Tax	.80
Atto Caldwell	4.00
	18.45
This Ticket	.35
	18.80

****

Johnson Vs. Wasson & McLelland
Civil Actions
Iredell County, NC [1861]

A Copy Delivered July 22nd 1861
W.F. Wasson, Shff

Messrs David Wasson & John O. McLelland.
    You are hereby notified that on the 17th August next at the house of Geo. L. Davidson in Lowndesboro, Lowndes County, Alabama, the depositions of George L Davidson, & Ross S. Davidson & others will be taken to be read in evidence in the Suit wherein Johnson & Co. are Plaintiffs & you are Defendants, pending in the Superior Court of Law for Iredell County, July 12th 1861
R.M. Johnson & Co. Plaintiffs
A Coppy Delivered Jany 22, 1861
W.F. Wasson, Shff

Iredell County
Civil Actions

State of North Carolina, iredell County.
    Know all Men by these Presents, That we J.O. McLelland, David A Wasson & W. Hains, all of the County aforesaid, are held and firmly bound unto WF Wasson, Sheriff of the County aforesaid, in the just and full sum of Five Thousand Dollars current money of the State aforesaid, to be paid unto the said W.F. Wasson, Shff his heirs, executors, administrators, or assigns, for the true performance whereof we bind ourselves, our heirs, administrators, executors, and assigns, jointly and severally, firmly by these presents. Sealed with our seals, and dated this 23 day of Mar A.D. 1861.
    The Condition of the above Obligation is such, That if the above bounden well and truly make their personal appearance at the next Superior Court to be holden for the County of Iredell on the 6th Monday after the 4th Monday in Feb next; then and there to answer unto R.M. Johnston, Hugh Reynolds & A.K. Simonton Traders under the name & stile of R.M. Johnson & Co. of a plea of breach of Covenant to Plaintiff Damage Twenty five hundred Dollars, and then and there to stand to and abide by the Judgment of said Court, and not depart the said Court without leave.
Signed, Sealed, and ordered in presence of:
J.O. McLelland   (Seal)
JA Wasson   (Seal)
WH Haynes   (Seal)

I, WF Wasson, Sheriff of the County of Iredell do hereby assign over the above Obligation and Condition to R.M. Johnson &C, the Plaintiff therein named, executors and administrators, to sue for and recover, agreeably to an Act of Assembly in such case made and provided.
Given under my hand and seal, this, the **[Blank]** day of **[Blank]** A.D. 1861
W.F. Wasson, Shff   (Seal)
Appearance Bond

State of North Carolina
To Hugh Kelly, a Justice assigned to keep the Peace in and for the County of Iredell -- Greeting:
    Know Ye, That we in confidence of your prudence and fidelity, have appointed, and by these presents do give unto You full power and authority, in pursuance of an order of our Superior Court of Law, made in a cause wherein Richard M Johnston & others are Plaintiffs against David Wasson & John O. McLelland, Defendants at such time and place as you

Iredell County
Civil Actions

shall think fit, to take, upon oath, the deposition of Joseph G. Eidson touchimg and concerning what he may know in and about the said controversy: and that you take such deposition in writing, and return the same closed up, under your hands and seals, to our said Court, to be held for the County of Iredell on the 6th Monday after the 4th Monday in August next, together with this Writ.
    Witness, R.A. McLaughlin, Clerk of our said Court, at Office, the 6th Monday after the 4th Monday in August A.D. 1861
R.A. McLaughlin, CSC

North Carolina }
Iredell County }

  At the Court House in Statesville on this 21st day of August 1862 in pursuance of a Commission to me directed from the Superior Court of Iredell County. I have called before me Joseph G. Eidson & having Sworn him in due form of Law to testify and declare what he might know touching a matter of controversy in a Suit pending in said Superior Court of Iredell Wherein Richard M. Johnson, Hugh Reynolds and AK Simonton are Plffs and John O. McLelland & David Wasson are Defendants, he testifyes and says as follows:

Question by Plff. Did you see & observe a negro boy in the possession of of R.M. Johnson & Hugh Reynolds to day.
Ans. I saw a negro boy by the name of Dick in their possession to day.

Question. How did it happen that you saw & observed said Slave today
Ans. Mr. Reynolds brought the boy into my room & asked me to look at him. I did look at him & examine his testicles, one of his testicles was three times as large as the other, the right testicle being the largest.

Question by Plaintiff. Did you see the boy pressing the contents of the right side of the scrotum upwards.
Ans. I did & the appearance of the boys Scrotum was considerably lessened but the right side still larger than the left.

Question by Plffs. When did you last see the boy Dick before today
Answer. I saw him the last time 1858 during the year I saw him several times.

Iredell County
Civil Actions

Question. Did you ever during the year 1858 observe any peculiar appearance about the body of the boy Dick if so how did you happen to see it and what was that Appearance
Ans. I & several others we went in swimming in 1858 & he got nearly drowned & we pulled him to the bank & then I saw his Scrotum & the right side was at least three times as large as the other or more.

Question. Did you and the others during that year while you were swimming

Question. By Pltff. Did you at other times in the year 1858 observe the boy? And what was the appearance of his scrotum
Ans. I was several times in swimming with the said boy during the year 1858 in the South Yadkin River near Baily's Mile and the appearance of the scrotum on the right side was more than three times as large as that on the left.

Question. Was the appearance of the scrotum to day when you examined him the same as when you saw it in 1858 as observation
Ans. Yes Sir

Question by Pltff. How does the appearance of the scrotum of the boy Dick as seen by you to day compare with its appearance in 1858 as you have before described.

The foregoing deposition of JG Eidson was taken and sworn to before me this day Aug 21st 1862 in the presence of both parties.
A Kelly, JP
J.G. Eidson, Deposition, Plff

State of North Carolina
Iredell County

Court & State aforesaid Justice of the Peace
    I Thomas A. James proceeded on the 6th day of November at L.Q. Sharpes Law Office in the town of Statesville on the day above read & both parties being present & the following witnesses were duly sworn & examined & testify as follows in the case of RM Johnson & Co. Vs JO

Iredell County
Civil Actions

McLelland & others. Cash Called and duly sworn by Defendant Deposeth and saith as follows:

Question by Deft. 1st. Did you know this Boy Dick about which this suit is brought if so state when you knew him & how long you new him & whether he was in any way injured if so state how
Answer. I think in fifty five & six I hired him, I never saw any thing the matter with him, he worked at all kinds of farm work and performed, it will in fact in three years heard any complaint from him.

Question 2nd by same. State what opportunities you had to Judge of his soundness and the dates
Answer. We were together for three years, I saw him in the creek at least half a dozen times naked, I did not see any thing the matter with his scrotum, I do not think that there was any thing the matter with it if there was, it was so small I could not see it

Q 3rd. State the last time you saw him and what was the matter with him at that time
Ans. I saw him after he was sold to the present Plaintiff and I heard of nothing wrong

Q. by Plff. Was the time you saw Dick as stated in your answer to the last question between the time the Plff bought him and the time of his being carried off to Alabama.
Answer. It was

Q2. Was it the night or in the day that you saw him or did you make any observation of the condition of his scrotum
Ans. It was in the night & I made no observation of his Scrotum

By Plff. Are you certain that you saw him in the creek washing in 1856 and you then gave attention to his scrotum
Answer. I saw him in washing in 1856 and gave no particular attention to his Scrotum but I saw nothing the matter with it

Q. by Plff. Have you judgment of the appearance of the affect of ruptures in these different conditions.
Ans. I do not know that I do but I have seen them rupture in different ways

Iredell County
Civil Actions

Q by Plff. Have you ever handled the scrotum of one that was Ruptured
Ans. I have not

By Deft. State what kind of Rupture this Boy Dick had
Ans. He had none when I saw him, if so, so small I could not discover it

Q By Plff. Are you a physician and did you examine the boy in view of ascertaining if he was Ruptured
Ans. I am not a physician and did not examine him with a view of ascertaining, but if there had been any thing of the kind I would have seen it. William Cash

---

T.A. James, JP
    After writing the above the Commissioners adjourned over to Friday the seventh of November for to examine Wm. F. Stone & R.A. Stone by consent of parties
    Parties not agreeable to adjournment & after having duly sworn W.F. Stone proceeded to take the following testimony.

Q by Defendant. Will you state if you know a boy by the name of Dick sold by the Defendants to the Plaintiff, if so state how long you knew him, and what was his condition as to soundness as regards his privates
Answer. He came to my Fathers in January of the year 58, he worked there in the Blacksmith shop untill he was sold [?]
Fall Term of Superior Court in the year 1859 on Tuesday of said Court, he was sold to R.M. Johnson & Co. as to his soundness I never knew anything wrong with him, I saw him the last time in Nov 59.

Q. State if you saw him during those two years - in a washing - in the River or Creek naked.
Ansr. I saw him in the River naked

Q. State what was the matter with his Scrotum - at the time you should have seen him in the River
Ansr. I saw nothing more the matter with him than there was with the others that was with him

Q. State what was the matter with the others that were with him
Ans. I did not see anything the matter with them-any of them

Iredell County
Civil Actions

Q. State the last time you saw him in the River naked - till the foresaid date you saw him the last time
Ansr. I do not know the precise date but it was in the summer of 59

Q. State what was the matter with his Scrotum at that time or any time previous to the last time you saw him in the River - naked
Ansr. I did not see any thing the matter with his scrotum at any time, I saw I, and did not see anything the matter with

Q. State with - Dick
Cross Examination reexamined by Plaintiff
Q. was the rock spoken of above or below the mill
Ansr. It was something like two hundred yards above the mill
W.F. Stone

Sworn to before me, Y.S. Dean, JP

R.A. Stone called by defendant duly sworn according to law deposeth saith as follows: as to wit
Q by Defendant. State what you know about the boy Dick, when you knew him the precise date, and the last knowledge of him - & what was the Circumstances under which you saw him the last time, particularly.
Answr. He (Dick) came to Fathers house, Eliza Stones, in January, 58, staid there untill Nov 1859 - I saw him working in the shop the last times as far as I know except he had the Mumps at one time, he was not bad with them, he didn't lye up with them, he had them for three or four days.

Q. by Defendant. State what the condition of the boy was last time you saw him, and under what circumstances you saw, when it was & where it was - & all about it
Answer. I saw him at South River - about the Bailey Mill - at a big rock at the washing place - the Saturday after he was sold - to the Plaintiffs, he stript off to go in a washing and went in - I did not see anything wrong with him

Q by Defendant. State whether or not if there had been any injury to his privates - if you could not have seen it

Iredell County
Civil Actions

Answer. Ever thing was right about them as far as I could see - he was as fast as a Rabit as far as I could see - if there had been anything wrong with him I could have seen it - I could have taken hold of him, he was near enough to me.

Q. by Deft. State if there was any enlargemt of the Scrotum the last time you speak of seeing him, in what year was it you saw him last
Answer. There was nothing wrong with him at that time - I saw him in the year 59 - on Saturday after the sale to the Plaintiff

Examination by Plaintiff

Q. Who were the persons composing the five to whom the negro was sold
Answer. Richard Johnson & A.K. Simonton & H. Reynolds - I suppose

Q. Who was present at the time you saw the negro Dick washing in the Mill pond or Creek, and who was in the creek or river with him
Answer. John W. Tase[?], David Sharpe & John Eidson & some black boys, Wm. Haynes was standing on the bank with me

Q. did you give more attention to the scrotum of Dick - than you did to the other boys that were in washing with him
Ansr. He was near to me than any of the others were, I could see him better

Q. were they not all washing together, mingling together while in the stream
Ansr. The others were in deep water while he was in shallow water, near the bank, he could not swim

Q. how far was the shallow water where Dick was from the rock
Ansr. It came up to the lower edge of the Rock

Q. State who was in the River with him the last time you speak of
Answer. I saw him in so often that I do not recolect who was in with him the last time

Q. State where it was you saw him in the River - naked - during that summer

Iredell County
Civil Actions

Ansr. I saw him in the River above the Bridge below the Baily Old Mills & at a Rock above the mills, as to how many times I do not know, of course he was naked when he was in a washing

Q. State who he belonged to - at the last time you so saw him
Answr. He belonged to McLelland & Wasson the last time I saw him

Q. did you give any particular attention to the Scrotum of Dick at that time
Ans. I do not think I saw them, the black boys went out on the other side of the River, and the white boys came out on the side I was on

Q. What month was it
Ansr. It was the time of the fall Superior Court of Iredell Co.

Q. how did it happen that you went up there that day
Ansr. I rode up to the Mill

Q. What relation are you to the Deft
Ansr. He Married my sister, that is all the relation

Examination resumed by Defendant

Q. state whether or not you noticed Dicks Scrotum on that occasion above spoke of, if so state what was the matter with it

Q. how far was Dick - and how far was the other boys from the Rock - where you was standing on it
Answer. Dick was on the Rock and went in off the rock, the other boys were in the River had been swimming - and was in the middle of the River when I went up there

Q. Was Dick in swimming with the other boys
Answer. No he was not

Q. Did you see the boys dress & undress
Answer. I did not see the other boys but saw them come out and dress, I saw Dick undress

Q. Did you give attention to the scrotum of the other boys
Ansr. They were in deep water & I could not see the other boys

Iredell County
Civil Actions

Q. How far were they from you when they came out and dressed
Ansr. It was some ten feet - probably, I did not notice it

Q8. Do you not think it was much as Eight or nine years
Answer. I cannot tell

Q9. Have you not said it was Eight or nine years
Ans. I have not to my recollection

Q10. Did you ever see him naked since you had him hired
Ans. No

By Deft. State when was the last time you saw him naked and washing in the creek
Ans. In the Summer of fifty six

Q2. By same. State what was the matter with the boy Dick at that time
Answer. I saw nothing the matter with him

Q 3rd. state if there had been anything the matter with his scrotum at that time if you could have seen it
Ans. Yes, if there had I could have seen it but there was nothing that I could see.

Quest 3rd at the times you stated in your answer to Deft 2nd question if having seen the boy naked what was he doing in the Creek
Answer. He was washing himself and playing in the Creek

Quest 4. Did you make any observation or turn your attention to see if there was any thing the matter
Answer. I did not turn my attention particular to see if there was any thing the matter or not but I was close enough at times to have haken hold of him

Q 5th was there anything peculiar with his Scrotum that attracted attention
Answer. I saw nothing more about him than other boys

Q 6th when you had once seen it did you have a curiosity to look at it again
Ans. I had not

Iredell County
Civil Actions

Q7. Was it the first year you hired him you saw it for the first time
Ans. Yes it was

Q8 how long was it from the time you first hired him till you last saw him
Answer. I cannot say

R.M. Johnston & Co. Vs Wasson & McLelland
Fall Term 1862

The Plff R.M. Johnson Speaketh & says the Plffs are not ready for the trial of this Suit for the absence of Ross Simonton, Drs McLelland & CC Haynes[?] by whom he expects to prove that the negro boy Dick sold by Defts to Plffs with Warranty of Soundness, for the breach of contract this Suit is brought [?] of April 1860 way sufficiency[?] by [?] of rupture Serious by impairing the Soundness & value of the Slave & that the rupture was one of long Standing before bringing to the date of the warranty that he gave the regular notice, to take the depositions in Lowndesboro in the State of Alabama 10th Sept ultimo & sent the Commissioner for that purpose to [?] agmt. At that place & said depositions have failed to arrive
R.M. Johnson
Sworn to and subscribed
RA McLaughlin, CSC

R.M. Johnson & others Vs Wasson & McLelland
Notice for depositions, August 12th 1862
A copy Delivered McLLin & Wasson
W.F. Wasson, Shff

Messrs David Wasson & John O. McLelland
You will take notice that on the 21st past and at the Court House in Statesville the depositions of Joseph G. Eidson, [?] H Eidson will be taken to be read as evidence on the Trial of the Suit pending in Iredell Superior Court Wherein Richard M. Johnson & others are Plaintiffs and you are Defendant - when & where you may attend & Cross Examine - August $9t^h$ 1862.
Richard M. Johnson & others, By Atto:

Iredell County
Civil Actions

R.M. Johnson & Co. Vs J.O. McLelland
A True Copy Delivered November 1st 1862
W.F. Wasson, Shff

State of North Carolina
Iredell County

R.M. Johnston & C O. Vs J.O. McLelland & D.A. Wasson

Mr. Hugh Reynolds
    Sir, as a member of the firm of R.M. Johnston & Co. I notify you that I shall proceed to take the Depositions of Wm. F. Stone & others at L.Q. Sharpes Law Office on the 6th of Nov 1862
J.O. McLelland.

Johnson & Co. Vs Wasson & McLelland
Notice for deposition, to Fall Term 1862
Executed july 28th 1862
By Delivery True copies of this notice to
DA wasson & John Mclelland
W Warren, Shff per WA Gurly, DS

Messrs David Wasson & John O. McLelland
    You are hereby notified that on the tenth day of Sept next at the house of George L. Davidson in the County of Loundes at Loundesboro in the State of Alabama the depositions of Geo. L. Davidson, Ross S. Davidson and others will be sent to be read as evidence on the trial in the Suit in the Superior Court of Iredell County wherein Richard M. Johnson, A.K. Simonton & Hugh Reynolds are Plffs and you are defendants when and where you may attend & Cross Examine.
R.M. Johnston & Co. by Atto.
July 15th 1862

State of North Carolina
To Thomas A. James & Y.S. Dean Justices assigned to keep the Peace in and for the County of Iredell.

Iredell County
Civil Actions

      Know Ye, That we in confidence of your prudence and fidelity, have appointed, and by these presents do give unto You full power and authority, in pursuance of an order of our Superior Court of Law, made in a cause wherein R.M. Johnston & Co. Plaintiff against John O. McLelland & David Wasson who are Defendants at such Time and place as you shall think fit, to take, upon oath, the deposition of William Cash, W.F. Stone, R.A. Stone & others touching and concerning what they may know in and about the said controversy, and that you take such deposition in writing, and return the same closed up, under your hands and seals, to our said Court, to be held for the County of Iredell on the 7th Monday after the 4th Monday in August next, together with this Writ.

      Witness, RA McLaughlin, Clerk of our said Court, at Office, the 6th Monday after the 4th Monday in August A.D., 1862.
Issued 6th Nov 1863
RA McLaughlin, CSC

State of North Carolina
To Charles S. Somers, Esquire, Justice assigned to keep the Peace in and for the County of Iredell Greeting:

      Know Ye, That we in confidence of your prudence and fidelity, have appointed, and by these presents do give unto You full power and authority, in pursuance of an order of our Superior Court of Law, made in a cause wherein Richard M. Johnston & Hugh Reynolds are Plaintiff against John O. McLelland & David A Wasson are Defendants at such time and place as you shall think fit, to take, upon oath, the deposition of W.H. Eidson touching and concerning what he may know in and about the said controversy: and that you take such deposition in writing, and return the same closed up, under your hands and seals, to our said Court, to be held for the County of Iredell, on the seventh Monday after the fourth Monday in August next, together with this Writ.

      Witness, R.A. McLaughlin, Clerk of our said Court, at Office, the Sixth Monday after the Fourth Monday in August A.D. 1862.
RA McLaughlin, CSC

State of North Carolina
To Thomas A. James, Esquires & Dr. Y.S. Dean, Justices assigned to keep rhe Peace in and for the County of Iredell -- Greeting:

Iredell County
Civil Actions

Know Ye, That we in confidence of your prudence and fidelity, have appointed, and by these presents do give unto You full power and authority, in pursuance of an order of our Superior Court of Law, made in a cause wherein R.M. Johnston & Co., Plaintiff against J.O. McLelland & D.A. Wasson are Defendants at such time and place as you shall think fit, to take, upon oath, the deposition of William Cash & others touching and concerning what he may know in and about the said controversy: and that you take such deposition in writing, and return the same closed up, under your hands and seals, to our said Court, to be held for the County of Iredell, on the sixth Monday after the Fourth Monday in August A.D., 1862
Issued 6th 1862
R.A. McLaughlin

State of North Carolina
To James K. Whitman, Commissioner and a Justice of the Peace, Esquire, Justice assigned to keep the Peace in and for the County of Lowndes, State of Alabama Greeting:
 Know Ye, That we in confidence of your prudence and fidelity, have appointed, and by these presents do give unto You full power and authority, in pursuance of an order of our Superior Court of Law, made in a cause wherein Richard M. Johnson & Hugh Reynolds are Plaintiffs against John McLelland and David Wasson, Defendants at such time and place as you shall think fit, to take, upon oath, the deposition of George Davidson, Dr. C.C. Howard & Dr. C. M. [?] touching and concerning what they may know in and about the said controversy: and that you take such deposition in writing, and return the same closed up, under your hands and seals, to our said Court, to be held for the County of **[Blank]** on the 7th Monday after the 4th Monday in August next, together with this Writ.
 Witness, RA McLaughlin, Clerk of our said Court, at Office, the 7th Monday after the 4th Monday in August A.D. 1863.
RA McLaughlin, CSC

N Carolina } Superior Court of Law
Iredell County }

Richard M. Johnson } Suit on
Hugh Reynolds } Covenant

Iredell County
Civil Actions

David A. Wasson Ag }
John O. McLelland }

In the above named Case the 25th day of July 1863 in presence of a Commission from our said Superior Court, in presence of both parties. Item [?] Eidson, of Law & testified as follows:

Question by Plffs. Are you acquainted with the negro, the subject of this Suit, if you are, how long have you known him, what is his name, & what is his age?
Ans. I have known the negro about five years, - his name is Dick, & is about twenty years of age as well as I can Judge at this time

Quest. Have you ever seen him in a situation so that you could judge of his form & make
Ans. I have seen him naked twice, from being in the River swimming with him.

Quest. Did you ever see anything peculiar or singular in any part of [?] if you did what was it
Answer. I did, one side of the bag or scrotum was enlarged near three times as large as the other side, & was of unnatural in size & shape - It was larger up at his bowels & tapered down to a point about 3/4 of an inch lower than the other side

Quest. Did anything happen to attract your attention if anything what was it
Ans. We went into the River washing & he got in a deep hole & came very near drowning & me & my Brother got him out, that was the first time I saw any thing the matter with him

Quest. What degree of attention did you give to his Scrotum at that time
Ans. I looked at it and was satisfied that it was three times as large as the other side.

Quest. When was it that you made this observation
Ans. In August 1858

Quest. How do you know that it was at that time

Iredell County
Civil Actions

Ans. I was working at Mr. Crouches making brick & my Father charged my work to Mr Crouch in his day book & it was in August 1858

Quest. What part of South River was it & who were with you at the time at the River
Ans. It was in Mr Keatons Bottom & there was no white person with me but my Brother Joseph, & three negro boys belonging to Silas Keaton

Quest. Was your attention ever turned to Dicks testicles or Scrotum at any other time
Ans. It was not, I never paid any attention to it at any other time

Quest. Did you ever see him naked at any other time
Ans. I did, & it was in the River above Mr Lawrence's Mill, I was in a washing & he come with some of Mrs Feinsters boys & they went in washing, I paid no attention to him at that time, this was in same year 1858 but later in the year, when I made the observation above stated

Quest. In whose possession was the boy in at the time you saw him in washing
Ans. He was in John O. McLellands possession

Quest. Do you know what became of the negro, how he was disposed of & to whom
Ans. Mr McLelland sold him to R.M. Johnston & Mr Hugh Reynolds in the year 1859.

Cross Examined by Defts

Quest. What day in the week was it that you & Dick went a washing
Ans. It was on Saturday evening on both occasions

Quest. How long was it after you saw the appearance of Dicks Scrotum before you spoke about it
Ans. About three years

Quest. Who did you speak to then about it
Ans. To Col. R M Johnson

Quest. How often have you & R M Johnson talked over this matter before

Iredell County
Civil Actions

Ans. Three times [?] as often as I recollect of having any talk to him about it.

Quest. Are you & R.M. Johnson very friendly
Ans. We are, I have no enmity at him & I don't suppose he has any at me

Quest. Are you on friendly terms with John O McLelland and Mr. Wasson
Ans. I have been ever since I first knew the men

Quest. Was the enlargement of Dicks Scrotum so that any body could see it plainly
Ans. It was, plainly to be seen

Quest. Is not every mans Scrotum one side larger than the other
Ans. What men that I have saw their testicles both sides are alike, unless diseased

Reexamine by Plff

Quest. How did you & Johnson first get into a conversation about this boy
Ans. He asked me if I had ever been in a washing with this boy. I told him I had

Quest. How come you to have three conversations with him about the boy Dick
Ans. The first time he asked me if I ever was in the water washing with Dick, I told him I was. He then asked me about his appearance - & I told him as near as I could, the next time he mentioned it to me he told me that he intended to have me & my Brother summond, that him & Mr Reynolds has a Law Suit with Mr McLelland & Wasson about the boy Dick - the third time he spoke to me about it, he told me he wanted our depositions take before we had to go to the Army

Quest. What was the reason your Depositions was not taken when your Brothers was
Ans. I was detailed to go to the Army & started on Tuesday before the deposition was to be taken on the next Thursday

The three last questions and answers are objected to by Defts
    His

Iredell County
Civil Actions

W X H Eidson
    Mark

The foregoing deposition of W.H. Eidson was taken & subscribed & sworn to before me this 25th day of July 1863 in the presence of both parties
C.S. Summers, JP

Johnson & Reynolds   }
Ag   }Deposition of W.H. Eidson
M McLelland & Wasson }

To the Clerk of the Superior Court of Iredell County

State of Alabama   }
Lowndes County   }

    In pursuance of a Commission issued to me from the Superior Court of Law of Iredell County, State of North Carolina I have on this 18th day of December 1863 at the house of James Whitman in the Town of Lownsboro in Lowndes County, State of Alabama Called before me George Davidson, Dr. C.C. Howard, Dr. C. McCrae
    And having sworn them in due form of Law to testify & declare such for himself what he might know of & touching the matter in controversy in the Suit pending in the Superior Court of Law for Iredell County, State of North Carolina, whereas Richard M. Johnson and Hugh Reynolds are Plffs & John O. McLelland and David Wasson are Defts, they testified & deposed as follows:
George Davidson Examined & deposeth as follows:

Question by Plffs. 1.st Did you know anything of a negro boy by name Dick brot to & sold in this place by Richard M. Johnson [?] if you do, state how you come to know him.
Answer. I do, R.M. Johnson & Co brought him here & I bought

Quest 2. When did you purchase said slave, about what was his age, where was he brought from, & what was his appearance as to Color, size & form of make?
Answer. I purchased him in Lowndesboro: about sixteen (16) years of age - rather chunky & copper Coloured and heavy set body

Iredell County
Civil Actions

Question 3rd How long did you own said boy Dick? What services & labour did you put him to?
Answer.   I owned him about 11 or 12 months and had him at the blacksmith business for which I purchased him for.

Question 4th Had he the skill in any business kinds formerly, if so what trade & what degree of skill in it did he possess?
Ans.   He had no particular skill as I know of - he was a sprightly boy & thought he would do for a striker in my black Smith shop

Question 5th What treatment as concerned his comfort & personal wellfare did he receive, while you owned him & as long as you had any knowledge of him?
Ans.   While in my possession he received as good treatment a negro generally get.

Question 6th What was the Constitution as to bodily Soundness of said boy while you owned him?
Ans.   Up to the time I discovered his unsoundness, which was rupture, he never lost a days work say for some 7 Months.

Question 7th How long after you purchased the said Dick before you discovered the defect in his Soundness as you have mentioned & what did you do, if anything, to satisfy yourself as to the nature and degree of the unsoundness of Sd boy?
Ans.   Some 7 or 8 Months after I discovered his unsoundness I called in 2 physicians, Drs. Howard & McCrae to examine him.

Question 8th Were you present when Dr. McCrae & Dr. Howard examined the boy & did they make a particular examination?
Ans.   I was present when Dr. Howard & McCrae which satisfied me they made a particular Examination

Question 9th How long have Dr. Howard & Dr. McCrae been in the professional practice of Medicine & what ere their standings as physicians?
Ans.   Dr. Howard about Twenty years & McCrae about thirteen years, and as good standing as physicians as any in the country

Iredell County
Civil Actions

Question 10th After you discovered the alleged unsoundness in the boy Dick what disposition did you make of him & what became of him & where was he the last you had any knowledge of him?
Ans. I took steps & did return him & went back to Iredell County, N.C. was there the last accounts

Question 11th If the boy Dick had been sound how much was he worth & how much was he worth in his actual condition as to his unsoundness?
Ans. I gave $1600 for Dick & thought him worth it. In his condition I should say about $800 price

The Examination of Dr. C.C. Howard

Question by Plff: How long have you been engaged in the professional practice of medicine Docter?
Ans. Upwards of twenty years in Alabama

Question 2nd Did you know anything of a negro boy named Dick owned by George Davidson & how did you come to have knowledge of him?
Ans. Mr Davidson requested me to see & examine the boy Dick which I did.

Question 3rd What examination did you make of said boy and what did you discover to be in this condition as to soundness? & what was the nature & degree of his unsoundness &? & the effect it would have upon his service & ability as a laborer?
Ans. I examined sufficiently to satisfy myself to know of him to have hernia which as well as I recollect was in groinal & reduceable

Question 4th What had been the duration of the unsoundness in your opinion and what grounds were there for [?] an opinion?
Ans. Probably of long standing. The size reducibility & freedom from any acute symptoms

Question 5th When was it you made an examination of said boy?
Ans. I think it was in the year of 1860

Examination of Dr. McCrae

Iredell County
Civil Actions

Question 1ˢᵗ   How long have you been in the professional practice of medicine & where?
Ans. Thirteen years in the States of N. Carolina & Alabama

Question 2ⁿᵈ   Did you know anything of a negro boy named Dick, owned by George Davidson, if so, how did you come to have any knowledge of him?
Ans. I do. I was Called professionable o by Mr. Davidson to Examine him.

Question 3ʳᵈ   What examination did you make of said boy? And what did you discover to be his condition as to unsoundness & what was the nature and degree of his unsoundness? & what effect would it have upon his ability & endeavour as a Labourer?
Ans. I made a thorough Examination. I discovered to be inguinal hernia. It would materially injure him as a labourer.

Question 4ᵗʰ   What in your opinion had been the duration of such unsoundness of Sd boy & why do you think so?
Ans. I should say of some time standing probably a year or more. I think so from the Size of it & the reducibility & [?] pain or active inflamation.

Question 5ᵗʰ   When was it you made an examination of said boy?
Ans. I think in the Fall 1860, Eighteen hundred and sixty.

The foregoing deposition of George Davidson of Dr. C.C. Howard & Dr. C. McCrae were taken, subscribed & sworn to before me at the Storehouse of James Whitman in the Town of Lownsboro in the County of Lowndes, State of Alabama the 18ᵗʰ Day of December 1863 -- Jas K Whitman

---

State of North Carolina   }
Iredell County   }

  Be it remembered that a Superior Court of Law was opened & held for the County of Iredell at the Court House in Statesville on the 2ⁿᵈ Monday after the 3ʳᵈ Monday in March AD 1870 the Honorable A. Mitchel, Judge of said Court present and presiding the following business was translated to wit

Iredell County
Civil Actions

R M Johnson }
Hugh Reynolds } Refered to JH McLaughlin
R.F. Simonton, Admr. } & AP Sharpe
Of AK Simonton }
Vs. } Award filed
John O. McLelland }
& DA Wasson } on Motion

    Judgment is rendered according to award for the sum of $500.00 [?] with [?] on the same from 6 Sept 1869 until paid, & it is further considered by the Court that the Plffs do cover of the Defts the Costs of the Suit sent in Court to be taxed by the Clerk

---

Superior Court of Law
Spring Term 1869

Richard M Johnson & Co } Genl issue 1969
Vs } performed no breach
John O. McLelland & }
David A Wasson }

    It is ordered by the Court that this Case be referred to John H Mclaughlin & AP Sharpe with leave to chose on umpire & their award to be a rule of Court - the writen testimony heretofore and hereafter to be taken to be read in evidence
C.S. Summers, Clk

R M Johnson & Co. Vs Jno O McLelland & DA Wasson

State of North Carolina }
Iredell County }

    This Case having been referred to the undersigned refferees whose award is to be a rule of Court which said award is as follows to wit

    We find the said boy Dick then a slave and the subject of this Controversy was unsound at the time of the sale we therefore fins in favor

Iredell County
Civil Actions

of the Plff, and assess their damage at five hundred dollars $500 in Currency. Given under our hands and seals this 6th day of Sept 1869.
A.P. Sharpe (Seal)
J.H. McLaughlin (Seal)

State of North Carolina
To the Sheriff of Iredell County, greeting:
    We command You, That of the goods and Chattles, Lands and Tenements, of John O. McLelland & D.A. Wasson if to be found in your County, you cause to be made the sum of $500 with interest on the same from the 6th day of September 1869 until paid which was lately in our Superior Court of Law held for Iredell County, at the Court-House in Statesville, adjudged RM Johnson, Hugh Reynolds & R.F. Simonton, Admr. of AK Simonton for debt, besides the further sum of $87.48 for costs and charges in the said suit expended, whereof the said defendants are liable, as appears to us of record. And have you the said monies, besides your fees for this service, before our said Court at Statesville aforesaid, on the 2n^d Monday after the 3rd Monday in August next, then and there to render the said debt, costs and charges aforesaid. Herein fail not, and have you then and there this Writ.
    Witness, C.S. Summers, Clerk of our said Court, at Office, the 2nd Monday after the 3rd Monday in March 1870. Issued June 1870.
C.L. Summers, CSC

No. 182
R.M. Johnson & Co. Vs J. O. McLelland & others
BK2, P 94
To Fall Term 1870
Satisfied, retained my fees & paid to office for debt & interest $39.68
W.F. Wasson, Shff

Deft J O McLelland to Officer 12 May 1870

$129.77
  90.23
$220.00   C.S. Summers, Clk

Judgment 4th April 1870

Iredell County
Civil Actions

Damages	500.00
Intr from 6 Sep 1869	
Writ Tax & Bond	2.40
16 Cont. 7 McL	4.80
9 Subp "	1.35
1 seal & postage "	.28
5 Commissions "	1.25
2 seals & Postage "	.56
1 Affidavit	.20
7 Subp	3.50
Order of Ref	.25
Transfering Cost	1.00
Judgment & Docketing	1.25
[?] Judgment	.25
DS WT Wtts	2.60
" WA [?]	1.20
" RO Linster	1.75
" SJ Rickert	.75
Shff Wasson	3.60
Att Beyden	4.00
	$50.99
R.F. Stone	4.88
J.F. Long	10.16
R.A. Stone	1.54
R.T. Campbell	1.74
M.T. Nesbit	1.90
J.G. Eidson	2.20
Dick Rumple	1.80
David Rumple	2.40
Silas Keaton	1.02
Jacob Parker	2.35
JW Tarp[?]	2.22
W.F. Crouse	7.94
W Cash	8.58
Elijah Stone	7.06
AP Sharpe, Ref	3.00
	89.78
This Fi Fa & L	.45
	90.23

Iredell County Civil Actions

****

R.M. Johnson Vs. A. Redman
Civil Actions
Iredell County, NC [1864]

R M Johnson Vs A Redman

This Case refered to J.F. Long, Silas Rector, JW Williams & O. Gillespie,
Parties Present
RM Johnson Plaintiff Caled Josep James after being qualified states as follows.

Question by Plaintiff. Are you acquainted with the negro boy now in Controversy
Ans. I am, I Carried him to Alabama for Plaintiff to sell & I sold him to a Man named Lindsay in Columbus, Ga for $900.00 & after he examined him he returned him to me stating that he would not have him on account of Sore on his leg Caused by a burn as he believed, I took him back & Carried him to West-Point- and sold him to a Man named Crowder for $900.00 who before Purchasing examined him & said he did not think it would hurt him he brot him back to me next day & said he wanted me to take him back as he had understood the Title to the boy was not good, I took him back & left him with Lee S. James taking his receipt for him to be delivered when called for

Question What is the difference you would have made in the boy the way he was or if he had been sound
Ans. A difference of from $75 to $100

Cross Question by Deft. Did you see the boy or not before I sold him to Plff, I did not and did not know whether the sore was there before he was sold or not

Question. Whether you think the scar that was would injure the negro from service or to his health in any way
Ans. My opinion is that it the sore was from a scar

Quest. How long did you have him in possession

Iredell County
Civil Actions

Ans. About two months

Quest. Did he not appear to be a sound boy when in your care see him limp or in any way deficient as you know before the first sale that any thing was the matter in any way
Ans. He did not

Question. Did Plff say any thing to you about the title of sd boy
Ans. I do not know how I heard but heard from some body

Question. What do you think the boy was worth or what would you have given for him the time you sold him last or the time you left him
Ans. $650.00

Question. How much would the boy hire for in Ala. Per month
Ans. I do not think he would hire for more than his victuals & clothes

Question by Plaintiff. How much were the necessary expenses of the boy while you had him
Ans. Thirty five 70/100 dollars

Dr. J.F. Long Question by Plaintiff. Was you or was you not with me at the time I purchased said negro
Ans. I was & wrote the bill of sale Plaintiff wished to see & examine the negroes defendant refused to show them giving as a reason that his wife was dissatisfied but said the negros were sound except the little girl who had an arm broken but it was entirely healed a few days after Plaintiff purchased said negros, he sent for me to go to his house & examine the negro boy, I did so & found he had a large scar on one of his legs caused by a burn.

Question by Defendant. Do you think the scar spoken of above would injure the boy in his work
Answer. It will not

Dr. WM Campbell Called by Plaintiff

Question. Did you not attend a negro girl belonging to Plaintiff named Minda

Iredell County
Civil Actions

Answer. I did, I saw the girl in November or December 1859 examined her arm & found a defect in the left arm Caused by fracture, her arm was considerably disfigured

Question by Plaintiff. As regards the scarr on the boys leg Caused by a burn likely to injure him in his work

Answer. It would not injure him in his work but if expanded in bad weather or any local injury to the burnt place would make a serious sore & a permanent injury

Dr. J. Howard Called by Plaintiff

Question. Did you not hear me propose to deliver said negros to A. Redman

Answer. I did

Witness Called for Defence, Silas keaton Called

Question. Do you know the girl in controversy & what did you think she was worth

Answer. I do, and think she was worth $700.00 Dollars say she was Sound

J W Williams Called by Defendant

Question. Do you know the negroes in Controversy

Answer. I do, I have known them ever since they were born, the boy I understood was burnt, I think the negroes at the time they were sold was worth $1500.00 if sound & so far as I know they were sound, I saw said negro Jack at West Point in Care of Jos James, he appeared well & active, James sold him at that place & afterwards took him back as the purchaser objected to the right but had no objection to the boy as to soundness, this scar spoken of by other witnesses was no objection to purchaser, I think the said boy was worth five Dollars pr month.

A K Simonton Called by Defendant

Question. Did you see the negro boy Jack in controversy in Alabama

Answr. I did, he appeared sound & well, Plaintiff sold said boy Jack for $1100.00 or there about

Iredell County
Civil Actions

Question by Plaintiff. Did you know the negro girl Mina in controversy if so describe the Condition of her arm.
Answr. I suppose I do there was a deficiency about her right arm, She did not have good use of it & I think it would injure the sale of said girl about fifty Dollars or More.

Alexander Redman Called by Defendant

Question. Do you know the negroes in Controversy & what oportunity had you of knowing them
Answr. I was raised with them, they were harty & sound, the boy Jack had a scar on his thigh caused by a burn, I don't think it injured him, I never heard the boy complain of the burn hurting him, I hoed corn with the Girl, she had good use of her arm, I don't know whether she could straten it or not, I think there was a little crook in it, don't know what caused it

John Redman Called by Defendant

Question. State what Johnson said as to the girls arm
Answr. Defendant told Plaintiff at the time of selling the girl had a deficient arm, the boy Jack was peart & active, he was considered Sound

Elbert Denny Called by Defendant

Question. Do you know the boy Jack in controversy, was he sound and active
Answr. I do, he was sound and active & one of the stoutest boys that Came to the [?].
1864

****

Tucker Vs Bobbit
Civil Actions
Iredell County, NC [1865]

On or before the 25th Dec 1865 I promise to pay T.S. Tucker three hundred Dollars common currency of the country for the hire of a negro girl Isabella. The said negro is to receive two full suits of clothes, one summer,

Iredell County
Civil Actions

one winter, One pair double soled shoes, One blanket or its equivalent, Pay all Taxes, State & Confederate
Witness my hand and Seal
Jan 2, 1865
S.H. Bobbit Jr.   (Seal)
S.H. Bobbit Senr.   (Seal)

State of North Carolina }
Iredell County   }

To any lawful officer to execute and return within thirty days from date hereof (Sundays excepted)

You are hereby commanded to take the bodies of S.H. Bobbitt Jr. and S.H. Bobbit Senr. Safely keep that you have them before me or some other Justice of the Peace for said County, to answer the complaint of T.S. Tucker for nopayment of the sum of three hundred dollars due by note.

Given under my hand and Seal, the 10th day of September 1866.
P.Tomlin, JP   (Seal)

I hereby deputise J.A. Baker to Execute and return according to Law
Sept. 10th 1866
P. Tomlin, JP   (Seal)

T.S. Tucker Vs S.H. Bobbit
Executed, J.A. Baker

Sept. 11th 1866 - Warrant returned parties present, Statements heard from each party - therefore it is adjudged that the Deft pay the Pltf on the obligation of Defts, therefore Judgment for Plff said obligations for the sum of forty dollars and Interest of the [?] coming of the Counts

Judgt.	40.00
From Which [?]	1.80
Judgment [?]	.80
	42.60

A.P. Sharpe, JP   (Seal)

Iredell County
Civil Actions

An appeal to the next Superior Court [?] 10 days to give security
18 Sept. 1866
C.W. Har[?]
P. Tomlin, JP

SH Bobbit Vs T.S. Tucker
FiFa, To Spring Term 1868
Bk 1, P 32

State of North Carolina
To the Sheriff of Iredell County, Greeting:
    We command you, that of the goods and chattles, lands and tenements of T.S. Tucker if to be found in your County, you cause to be made the sum of $8.25, which was lately in our Superior Court of Law, held for the county of Iredell at the Court House in Statesville adjudged S.H. Bobbit $8.25 cents for debt, besides the further sum of $8.25 for costs and charges on the said suit expended, whereof the said TS Tucker is liable, as appears to us of record. And have you the said monies, besides your fees for this service, before our said Court, at Statesville aforesaid, on the 7th Monday after the last Monday in February next, then and there to render the said debt, costs and charges aforesaid. Herein fail not, and have you then and there this Writ.
    Witness C.S. Summers, Clerk of our said Court, at Office, the 7th Monday after the last Monday in August 1867.
C.L. Summers, Clerk
Issued 10 February 1868.

Entering appeal	1.00
Appeal Tax	.80
2 Cont	..60
Judgment & Bill	1.10
Const J A Baker	.40
Atto	4.00
	7.90
This Ticket	.35
	8.25

Iredell County
Civil Actions

****

Morgan Vs. Colvert
Civil Actions
Iredell County, NC [1872]

B Morgan Vs. Robert Colbert
Order to sue in Term [?]

North Carolina }
Iredell County }

  Personally appears before me, Bartlet Morgan, & maketh oath that, as he is informed & believes, he hath a good Cause of return against Robert Colbert, in regard to a negro slave that said Colbert wrongfully took from him whilst it remained a slave & applicants property. That applicant is a poor person with but little property of any kind, unable to make the deposit required by law to entitle him to a Summons, that he has made diligent and long -- continued effort to give Security for the required undertaking for a Summons, & is utterly unable to do so
B Morgan

Sworn to & subscribed before me this the 21st Feb AD 1872
CS Summers, CSC

I certify that I have examined into the Cause of action mentioned above & believe that petitioner B Morgan has a good Cause of return
Feb 21st 1872
R.G. [?]

Chambers in Statesville Feb 20th 1872, the Clerk of the Superior Court of Iredell County will issue Bartlet Morgan such Summons as his case may require, against Robert Colbert without requiring any undertaking or deposit from him
A. Mitchell, Judge

Bart. Morgan Vs. Robert S. Colbert
Spring, Iredell
Feby 23rd 1872, a coppy Delivered

Iredell County
Civil Actions

W.F. Wasson, Shff
Iredell, Armfield

Iredell County: In the Superior Court, Bartlet Morgan against Robert S. Colbert.

State of North Carolina,
To the Sheriff of Iredell County--Greeting:

You are hereby Commanded to Summon Robert S. Colbert the Defendant above named, if he be found within your County, to be and appear before the Judge of our Superior Court, at a Court to be held for the County of Iredell at the Court House in Statesville on the 2nd Monday after the 3rd Monday of March next, and answer the complaint which will be deposited in the office of the Clerk of the Superior Court of said County within the three first days of said Term, and let the said Defendant take notice that if he fail to answer the said complaint within that time, the Plaintiff will apply to the Court for the relief demanded in the complaint.

Hereof fail not, and of this Summons make due return.
Given under my hand and seal of said Court, this 21st day of Feb. 1872
C.S. Summers, Clerk

Iredell County
Miscellaneous Records

Chapter Three

Iredell County

Miscellaneous Records

North Carolina State Archives
Iredell County Records
Records of Slaves and Free Persons of Color
C.R.054.928.2

Regulations Concerning Slaves

Ring the Court House Bell at 10 oclock every night and at all other times when necessary to alarm the Citizens absent from home. Arrest all Slaves after the Bell rings and after the Calaboose is finished lock them up till day light. Give them 15 lashes and inform the magistrate of their names & owners. Accept no pass unless the place or places where the Slave is permitted to go is written in the same -- & arrest the Slave if found off a direct line & road from one place to another. Arrest all Slaves engaged in a disturbance with or without a pass. A pass allowing a Slave to Visit his wife is good for one month and then must be taken up and another given or he will be Arrested. Any White person guilty of making a disturbance or other Conduct Calculated to disturbe the Citizens will be requested to stop & his name will be reported to the Magistrate next day in order to have him Arrested by the Constable.

Iredell County
Miscellaneous Records

Calvin Perry is the man the meat belongs to
Ebenezer McNeily, Cowan Chambers to prove by
T.A. Allison, J.F. Bell, E.B. Stimpson, Matthias Boger, Thos Templeton, J.W. Williams, [Faded] Scroggs, Jno Davidson, Jno Ga[?]ing, W.D. Hull, Thos Watts & W.J. Brawley

****

J.O. McLelland & D. Wasson
Bill of sale, 1859
Rec'd of Johnson Simonton Thirteen Hundred dollars in full payment for a negro Boy named Dick aged about Fifteen years, which Boy we Warrant to be sound in body and mind & we Warrant the Title to said Negroe and sell him as a slave for life
J.O. McLelland (Seal)
D.A. Wasson (Seal)
October 4th 1859, Witness O. Gillespie

****

Coroner's Returns
Inquest, Metmoth, a Slave, 1858

State of North Carolina }
Iredell County   } We the Jurors

Being summoned and Sworn proceeded to examin the body of Melmoth a Negro Slave belonging to Mr. E. Monson late of this County and are satisfied that he came to his Death by Hanging by his own hand
W.T. Gaither, Enens Gaither, G. Gaither, M. Gaither, J.N. Gaither, A.J. Gaither, Nelson Forcum[?], D.M. Campbell, J.B. Forcum, H. Tomlinson, J.W. X Campbell & G.W. Boley
Test.
J.E. Montgomery, Coroner

****

Report of Inquest of Delia
Property of Mrs. J.M. Reid

Iredell County
Miscellaneous Records

State of North Carolina }
Iredell County   }

  According to authority given to me [?] special Coroner I proceeded with the Undersigned Jurors Who were sworn to in [?] the case of the suden death of a slave Delia the property of Mr JM Reid on this day and after examining the Witnesses upon oath do find the following verdict viz that the said slave Delia came to her death by the accidental stroke of a knife in her own hand

J.B. Kerr, Coroner

Jurors: Wm o'k[?], RR Templeton, Edw Hales, Thos M. [?], Joseph L. Rumple, D.C. Thorn, James Shepherd, JW Brawley, W.K. McNeely, [?] T. Neill, A.M. [?]

Iredell County
Petitions to Sell Slaves

Chapter Four

Iredell County

Petitions to Sell Slaves

North Carolina State Archives
Iredell County Records
Records of Slaves and Free Persons of Color
C.R.054.928.2

Petitions to Sell Slaves

Order
Sale of David Boleys negroes by H. Forsyth
Commissioner on the 11th day of Sept 1841
Confirmed Feby 1842

North Carolina   } County Court
Surry County   } Aug Term 1841
Adlai Beard & others }

    Petition for sale of slaves - ordered by the Coourt that Henderson Forsyth be appointed Commissioner to make sale of the Slaves mentioned in the Petition; that public advertisement at three public places be made of

Iredell County
Petitions to Sell Slaves

the Sale for 20 days, that the Sale be made at Absalom Robeys Storehouse for twelve months credit with bond & good Security that the Commissioner appropriate & divide the bonds or proceeds of the Sale among the Petitioners according to their respective rights, Report to the next Court.
Test
J.F. Alexander, Clk

In pursuance of the above order I caused the said Slaves to be sold at - A Robeys Esqrs 11 Sept 1841 - Sale was as follows to

Harison H Davis Mimi & Child	$600.50
James M Baily Elizabeth	507
	$1107.50

Cont Paid of the following Claims	
Adlai Beard & Wife	215.17
Alexander Baily Gard (Cynthia & Elon	430.34
JM Baily	123.18
Jane Baily	20.28
Joseph Caldwell Gar Thomas	194.45
A Beard for advance	106.98
Sheriffs Recpt, Int & Court costs	17.10
	$1107.50

H. Forsythe, Comm

****

J.R. Simonton & others, Ex Parte
Petition to sell a slave
Report of Sale

North Carolina }
Iredell County }

In this case J.R. Simonton the Commissioner appointed to sell the Slave mentioned in the Petition respectfully reports that after giving the Lawful notice at 4 public places in Sd County, he sold the negro Boy Jesse mentioned in the Petition & upon a Credit of 6 months with interest from Date & that Hugh Reynolds became the purchaser at the sum of Twelve Hundred & Thirty seven Dollars & Bond & approved surety taken

Iredell County
Petitions to Sell Slaves

J.R. Simonton
By Attorney

****

Sales of Buonaparte J. Brevard's Negroes

A return of the Sales of Buonaparte J. Brevard property on the 8th August 1823 at 12 months Credit. To Wit.

1 Negro Man named Frederick
sold to Thomas M. Even			$500

1 Negro Girl Preedy to
John Davidson				372

****

J.M. Turner & others
Report of Sale
Decree of Court

State of N Carolina   } Co. of Pleas Q Sessions
Iredell County   } August Term 1860

J.M. Turner & others   } Petition for Sale of
Ex Parte   } a slave for partition

J.M. Turner the Commissioner appointed for the purpose reports that he has sold the said Slave mentioned in the Plaintiffs petition after giving twenty days notice at three public places in Sd County, That Sd Slave was sold publicly & that James Kelly became the purchaser at the sum of 1201 which sd money has been paid to your Commissioner
J.M. Turner, Commr., By Attorney

Whereupon it is ordered adjudged & decreed that the said commissioner after first paying the cost of this suit & also after deducting the sum of ten Dollars which is hereby allowed him for his Sale & report proceed to dispose of the resident as follows to wit $400.33 1/3 cts thereof to the Petitioner James A. Tucker & $400.33 1/3 cts thereof to the Petitioner

Iredell County
Petitions to Sell Slaves

Nancy Tucker & $400.33 1/3 cts thereof to him her the sd Lassiter[?] as Grounds of Mrs [?] Tucker & further that said Commissioner make a title to the purchaser of said Slave.
JM Turner, by Attorney

Appendix A
Glossary of Legal Terms

Appendix A

Glossary of Legal Terms

[Definitions of legal terms appearing in transcriptions within this book are derived from *Black's Law Dictionary*.]

Affidavit: A voluntary declaration of facts confirmed by the oath of the individual making it.

Agent: An individual authorized by another to act in place of another person.

Alias Capias: the issuance of a second writ.

Calaboose: An old term for jail or prison. From the Spanish word, "*calabozo.*"

Certiori: A writ issued by a superior court to an inferior court for the purpose of an investigation into irregularities.

Diminution of the Record: A phrase stating that the record delivered from an inferior court to a superior court for review is incomplete.

Execution: The carrying out of an act to its completion.

Ex Parte: Done for, or on the application of, one party only.

Fi Fa (Fiere Facias): A writ requiring a sheriff to satisfy a judgment levied from a debtors property.

Appendix A
Glossary of Legal Terms

Nol Pros (Nolle Prosequi): The prosecuting attorney will no longer prosecute the case.

Recognizance: An obligation of an individual, before a magistrate, that he will perform some act required by law

Solicitor: The chief law officer in a governmental body.

Special Venire: To appear in court, or citizens from whom a jury is selected. A Special Venire is usually called for a protracted case.

Subpoena: An order to appear at a specific and time to testify upon a certain matter.

Surety: An individual who is primarily liable for payment of debt, or for the performance of obligation of another.

Writ of Detinue: An order to recover, in specie, the property or chattels from an individual who acquired them lawfully, but retains the property without lawful right, with compensation for the detention.

Venire Facias: A writ directed to the sheriff to command that he cause twelve good and lawful men to come to court on a given day to serve as jurors.

Trespass: The unlawful interference with another's rights or property.

True Bill of Indictment: An endorsement issued by a grand jury upon finding sufficient evidence for a criminal charge.[4]

---

[4] Henry Campbell Black, M.A., ***Black's Law Dictionary***, 6th ed. (St. Paul, Minn: West Publishing Company, 1990)

Table of Cases
Civil and Criminal Actions

Table of Cases

Civil and Criminal Actions

Cases

Carleton Vs. Bell
Civil Actions
Iredell County, NC [1856]_____ 79

Cavin Vs. Long
Civil Actions
Iredell County, NC [1859]_____ 109

Johnson Vs. Wasson & McLelland
Civil Actions
Iredell County, NC [1861]_____ 136

Kelly Vs. Johnson & Carmichael
Civil Actions
Iredell County, NC [1859]_____ 86

M. L. Nesbet Vs Jacob Ramsour
Civil Actions
Iredell County, NC [1860]_____ 133

Morgan Vs. Colvert
Civil Actions
Iredell County, NC [1872]_____ 166

Table of Cases
Civil and Criminal Actions

Parks Vs. Smith
  Civil Actions
  Iredell County, NC [1856] _____ 84

R.M. Johnson Vs. A. Redman
  Civil Actions
  Iredell County, NC [1864] _____ 160

State Vs S.D. Chipley
  Criminal Actions
  Assaulting a Slave Girl
  Iredell County, NC [1864] _____ 73

State vs. Amos Jacobs
  Criminal Actions
  Trading with Slaves
  Iredell County, NC [1858] _____ 42

State Vs. Andrew Kerr
  Criminal Actions
  Trading with Slaves
  Iredell County, NC [1856] _____ 30

State Vs. Andrew Kerr
  Criminal Actions
  Trading with Slaves
  Iredell County, NC [1863] _____ 58

State Vs. Andy, a Slave
  Criminal Actions
  Rape
  Iredell County, NC [1866] _____ 76

State Vs. B.B. Lundy
  Criminal Actions
  Trading with Slaves
  Iredell County, NC [1860] _____ 45

State Vs. Bill Jones, a Free Negro
  Criminal Actions

Table of Cases
Civil and Criminal Actions

Assault & Battery
Iredell County, NC [1860] _____ 44

State Vs. Dick, a Slave
Criminal Actions
Burglary
Iredell County, NC [1864] _____ 64

State Vs. Hugh, Frank & Buck, Slaves
Criminal Actions
Burglary
Iredell County, NC [1863] _____ 52

State Vs. Ike, a Slave
Criminal Actions
Arson
Iredell County, NC [1864] _____ 69

State Vs. Isaac, a Slave
Criminal Actions
Arson
Iredell County, NC [1864] _____ 60

State Vs. M.E. Heyanis
Criminal Actions
Trading with Slaves
Iredell County, NC [1864] _____ 58

State Vs. Marlow
Criminal Actions
Assisting a Slave to Escape
Iredell County, NC [1855] _____ 25

State Vs. Rufus, a Slave
Criminal Actions
Theft
Iredell County, NC [1855] _____ 20

State Vs. Tom, (a Slave)
Criminal Actions

Table of Cases
Civil and Criminal Actions

Attempted Rape
Iredell County, NC [1853]_____ 1

State Vs. Wilson, a Slave
  Criminal Actions
  Murder
  Iredell County, NC [1858]_____ 34

State Vs. Wm. Ballard, Jr.
  Criminal Actions
  Trading with Slaves
  Iredell County, NC [1860]_____ 50

Tucker Vs Bobbit
  Civil Actions
  Iredell County, NC [1865]_____ 163

Young Vs Mills
  Civil Actions
  Iredell County, NC [1861]_____ 135

Index

Index

A

Absher
　John A., 91
　John L., 91
　Walter, 91
Alabama Counties
　Loundes, 147
　Lowndes, 136,
　　149, 153, 156
Alabama Towns
　Loundesboro, 147
　Lowndesboro,
　　136, 146, 153
　Lownsboro, 156
　West Point, 61
Alexander
　Charles T., 17
　Chs. T, 8
　J.F., Clk, 174
　T N, Shff, 3
　T.N., 2, 14
　T.N., Shff, 5, 14
　Thomas N, Shff, 18
　Thomas N., Sheriff, 9
　Thomas N., Shff, 17
　Thos. N., Shff, 8

TN, Shff, 4, 7, 10, 11, 17
Allen
　H E, 27
　H.E., 28, 29
　H.E., JP, 29
Allison
　Franklin, 36
　J.S., Foreman, 65, 68, 72
　Joseph, 31
　JS, Foreman, 73
　Miss Nancy, 37
　Nancy, 35, 37, 38, 41
　R.M., 32
　R.M., Solicitor, 31
　T.A., 31, 170
　TC, 13
　Thomas A., 25
　Wm M, 39, 40
Altra
　BC, 42
Amos
　Johnson, 22
Anderson
　Abel, 55
Armfield
　R.F., Solicitor, 56, 65, 73

RF, Solicitor, 68, 72
Atwell
　Benjamin, 32
Austin
　H R, 52
　H R, Clk, 53
　H.R., 52
　H.R., Clerk, 55
　H.R., Clk, 53, 56
　H.R., CSC, 53, 54, 57, 87
　HR, CSC, 89

B

Bailey
　John L., Judge, 55
　Saml., 89
Baily
　Alexander, 174
　James M., 174
　Jane, 174
　JM, 174
Baily Old Mills, 144
Baily's Mile, 139
Baker
　J.A., 164
　J.A., Constable, 165
Ballard

183

Index

William, 51
William S., 50
Wm. S., 50
Wm., Junr., 51
Bank of Cape Fear, 34
Bankes
  John, 55
Barker
  John, 108
Barnet
  David W, 8, 17
  David W., 17
Bass
  E., 112
  Ezekiel, 120, 129
Beard
  A., 174
  Adlai, 173, 174
Bell
  J F, 80, 82
  J F, Senr., 83
  J.F., 79, 80, 81, 82, 170
  J.F., Junr., 81
  JF, 80, 82, 83
  JF, Senr., 81
Bellevue Hospital, 88, 98, 99, 102
Bellevue Hospital, in Richmond, 105
Bellevue Hospital, in Richmond Virginia, 88
Berryhill
  J.J., 17
  JJ, 8
  Pinckney, 11
  Pinkney, 11
  Wm., 10
Blackburn
  W.H., 57
  William, 56

Boarding House of James A. Kelly, 90
Bobbit
  S.H., 164, 165
  S.H., Junr., 164
  S.H., Senr., 164
  SH, 165
Bobbitt
  SH, Junr., 164
Boger
  Matthias, 170
Boley
  David, 173
  G.W., 170
Bolton
  Dr., 99
Booe
  John C, 57
  John C., 56
  Wm E, 89
  Wm. E., 89
Bottom
  James, M.D., 88
Bowman
  R.O., 120
Boyd
  Thos S., 11
  Thos. S., DS, 10
Branley
  J.M., 40
  JM, 36
  John M., 36
Brawley
  J.W., 171
  John, 34
  W.J., 170
Brawly
  JM, 120
Brevard
  Buonaparte J, 175
  Buonaparte J., 175
Brinkle
  John, 55

Brogden
  Thos, 52
  Thos., 52
Brown
  Jackson, 93
  Jane, 81
  R., 30
  R.C., 33
  Robert, 30
  Robert C., 31
  Robt., 34
  Thomas S., 31
  Wm., 17
Browne
  Wm., 8
Browns
  R.O., 131
Bryan
  Wm., 92

C

Cabell
  Dr., 94
Cain
  P.H., 55
  P.H., Foreman, 56
Calaboose or Jail, 169
Caldwell
  Joseph, 174
  JW, Clk, 118
  JWP, Clk, 109, 113
  W P, 120, 133
  W P, Clk, 124, 125, 127
  W P, CSME, 125
  W.P, JP, 118
  W.P., 43, 119, 129
  W.P., Clk, 127
  W.P., CSC, 123, 132

Index

W.P., Esqr., 129
WP, 111, 123
WP, JP, 126
Callaway
  James, 85, 86
  James:, 86
Calloway
  Jas., 92
Cambill
  S.J., 106
Campbell
  D.M., 170
  Dr. R.T., 38, 40
  Dr. W.M., 44, 161
  E.M., 83
  EM, 83
  George, 8, 17
  H.M., 81
  J.W., 170
  M., 21, 25, 31, 40
  M., Foreman, 29, 45
  M., JP, 34
  R.T., 159
Cannon
  Henry G, 96
  Henry G., 105
  Henry G., Attorney, 95
Carleton
  M L, 80, 81
  M.L., 79, 81, 82
  ML, 80, 82
  P, 129
Carlton
  C.A., 124, 130
  C.A., D Clk, 4, 5
  M L, 83
  M.L., 82
  P.C., 37, 113, 120
Carmichael
  A B, 87, 89, 92, 94, 95, 106, 108

A.B., 86, 88, 89, 91, 92, 93, 94, 106
AB, 87, 90, 91, 92, 94, 95, 106, 108
L.B., 85, 86
LB, 86
W.W., 95
Carson
  Robert, 56, 57
  Robt., 53
Cash
  W., 159
  William, 141, 148, 149
Cashion
  JD, 13
Cathey
  G.C., 17, 18
  GC, 8
  George C., 8
Caughran
  Wm, 46, 49
  Wm., 45, 46, 48
Caughron
  William, 45
Cavin
  Eliza, 109, 113, 115, 118, 119, 123, 124, 125, 126, 127, 128, 129, 132
  John, 120, 129
  Mary, 120, 130, 131
  Miss, 109, 110, 113, 114, 115
  Miss Eliza, 126
  Mrs. Eliza, 126
  Sarah, 119, 123, 127
Cavins
  Eliza, 110, 119
  Miss Eliza, 112

Chamberlain
  Saml., 36
Chambers
  C., 37
  Cowan, 38, 170
  R.C., 36, 39, 40
Chatham
  J.K., 13
Chipley
  George W, 23
  Isabella, 79
  Mrs., 84
  S.D., 73, 75
  S.D.W., 75
  SD, 74, 75
  Simp, 75
  Simps, 73, 76
  Simpson, 74
Chiply
  G.W., 22
Clark
  A., 133
  Alex, 117, 131
  Alexander, 125, 126
  Alexr., 130
Clement
  JM, Attorney, 94
Clodfelter
  Solom, 130
Clouse
  William, 55
Cobb
  John N., 87, 94
Cockran
  William, 47
Colbert
  Robert, 166
  Robert S, 167
  Robert S., 166, 167
Cook
  H, 52
  H., 52
  H., JP, 53

Index

Cooper
  Alexander, 8, 17
  T C, 54
  T.C., 54
Cornatzer
  Jacob, 55
Costner
  Wm., 47
Cowan
  W.F, JP, 67
  W.F., 25
  W.F., JP, 21
  WF, 21
  WF, JP, 21, 61
  Wm. F., 38, 40
Cowles
  A.E., 56
  Josiah, 57
Crenshaw
  Dr., 88, 94, 102, 103, 105
  Dr. O.A., 87, 88, 98, 105
  O.A., 87, 95
  O.A., M.D., 88, 102
Critz
  H, 57
  H., 56
  Haman, 56
Crouch
  Mr., 151
Crouse
  W.F., 159
Cuthrell
  James N., 55
  Joseph F., 55

D

Dalton
  J.H., 52, 57
  John H, 52
Daniel

Wilson C., 55
Davidson
  Geo L., 136
  Geo. L., 147
  George, 149, 153, 155, 156
  George L, 136
  George L., 147
  Jane, 80
  Jno., 170
  John, 25, 31, 175
  Mr., 155, 156
  R F, 6, 7, 18
  R.F, 9
  R.F., 6, 7, 10, 12, 15
  RF, 7, 9, 10, 16, 19
  Robert F, 2, 9, 14, 18
  Robert F., 1, 6, 18, 19, 20
  Robt., 6
  Robt. F., 10
  Ross S., 136, 147
  T.F., 119, 126
  Theophilus F., 125
  Tho. F., 118
Davis
  Geo. C., 53
  Harrison H., 174
  Hecter, 94
  Hector, 87, 88, 96, 97, 98
  Hector, Auction House of., 96
  Hector, Auction Store of., 97
  Hector, Store of on Franklin Street, in Richmond, Virginia, 87
  Mr., 97, 98

R.A., 94
R.H., 88, 98
Robert H, 87
Robert H., 87, 95, 96, 105
Deadman
  George, 55
Dean
  Dr. Y.S., JP, 148
  Y.S., JP, 142, 147
  Yancy, JP, 124
Denny
  Elbert, 163
Dick
  John M., Judge, 8, 17
Diseases
  Abcess, 101
  Consumption, 103
  Hernia, 155
  Mumps, 142
  Pleurisy, 100
  Venereal Disease, 110
  Whooping Cough, 99
  Whooping-Cough, 101
Dockery
  Saml., 36, 38, 40, 46, 48
  Samuel, 42, 43, 46
Dodge
  Jas R, Clk, 15
Donaldson
  J.S., 50
  Ja., JP, 50
  John S, 50
  John S., 50
Donalson
  J.S., JP, 50
Donelson
  J L, 51
  J.L., 51

Index

Dowell
  Joshua, 36, 38
Draky
  Samuel, 45

E

Eaton
  Benjamin H., 55
  Jacob, 55
  Jesse T., 55
Eccles
  H.C., 65
Edsen
  CM, 69
  Morman, 67
Eidsen
  Morman, 72
Eidson
  J.G., 139, 159
  John, 143
  Joseph G, 138, 146
  Joseph G., 138
  Morman, 70
  W H, 153
  W H., 148, 153
Ellis
  Isham P., 55
Erwin
  A.R., 8, 17
  AR, 17
  E.W., 58
Even
  Thomas M., 175

F

Feinster
  Mrs., 151
Feraby
  Daniel, 38
Flanniken

Samuel, 8, 17
Fleming
  J. M. M., 59
  M. M., 59
  Mont., 59
Fletcher
  James, 32
Forcum
  J.B., 170
  Nelson, 170
Forsyth
  H., 173
  Henderson, 173
Forsythe
  H.,
  Commissioner, 174
Fraley
  Jacob, 36, 38, 40
Freeland
  A., 37
  Allison, 34, 37
  Anderson, 40
  Andrew, 38
  M. Franklin, 37, 38
  M.F., Clk, 25, 43
  Margaret, 35, 41
  MF, Clk, 32
  Milas F., 25
  Miles F., 80
  Mrs., 35
  Mrs. Margaret, 37
  Sarah, 81
  Silas, 80
  W.A., 38
  WA, 37
Freelands
  Mrs., 35
Freland
  Franklin, 40
  M F, 36
  M. Franklin, 36
  M.F., 40
  Margaret, 41

W.A., 40
Furches
  Thomas, 55

G

Gaines
  Thomas, 77
Gaither
  A.J., 170
  Basil, 55
  Enens, 170
  G., 170
  Ivy, 32
  J.N., 170
  Leander, 32
  M., 170
  Milton, 55
  W.T., 170
Gaithers
  Amos, 54
Gardner
  Graften, 134
Georgia Towns
  Columbus, 160
Gibson
  Morman, 65
  Thomas, 17
  Thos, 8
Gillaspie
  J.P, JP, 11
  JP, 11
Gillespie
  O., 170
  Otho, 59
  R.L., 32
  R.S., 30, 34
  Robert L., 30
  RS, 33
Gilreath
  B.C., 94, 95
  BC, 91
Gordon
  J.B., 86

Index

JB, 85
Gourney
  Thomas, 36
Grant
  Duffy, 70
  Moore, 66
  R.M., JP, 60, 67
  RM, JP, 60, 61, 67
Gray
  Joseph, 29, 30
  Wm., 8, 17
Greer
  E.C., Shff, 11, 13, 16
  EC, 12
Grey
  Jos., 29
Gribble
  Mary, 2, 9
  Mary A, 1, 9, 10, 18
  Mary A., 1, 9, 13, 18, 20
  Miss, 2
  William, 18
  Wm., 9, 10
Gribbles
  Wm., 13
Griffeth
  Robert, 55
Gurly
  W.A., DS, 147
Gurney
  James M., 36, 39
  M., 36
  Thomas, 39
  W., DShff, 37
  W.A., 38
  W.A., DS, 71
  William, 65, 67
  William A, 72
  William A., 65, 72
  Wilson, 38

Wm A, 66
Wm A, DS, 66, 70, 71
Wm. A., DS, 66
Gurny
  W.A., DS, 60

H

H.S. Shuford & Co, 111
Hackett
  R.F., 86
  RF, 91
Hainline
  N., 89
  Nathan, 89
Hains
  W., 137
Hales
  Edw., 171
Hall
  Daniel, 91
  Edwin, 63
  Franklin, 89
  John, 88, 91, 92, 99
  Mary, 82
  Mr., 97, 99, 102, 105
  Mr. John, 96, 97
  Saml. B, 18
  Saml. B., 8
  Samuel B., 8
  William, 92
  Wm., 91, 92
Hampton
  Agnes R, 66
  Agnes R., 65
  Agnes Rebecca, 65, 68
  J.W., 67
  JW, 67
Hanes

John H., 55
John N., 55
Harbin
  A.A., DC, 52, 54, 57
Harden
  Andrew J., 50
Hardin
  Andrew J, 50
Harris
  S.A., 5
  Samuel A, 7
  Samuel A., 5, 6
Hause
  Franklin, 22
Haynes
  CC, 146
  W H, 137
  Wm., 143
Hector Davis
  Store of, 95
Heganus
  M.E., 59
Hege
  Jno., 55
  John, 55
Helper
  H P, 51
  H R, 50
  H.P., 50
  Pinkney, 51
Henderson
  David M., 8, 17
  DM, 17
Heyanis
  M.E., 58
  ME, 59
Hill
  Archibald, 16
  Henry, 62, 70, 72
  J. Henry, 66
  M.W., 63, 68
  Martha, 70
  Miles, 72
  Milus, 70, 72

Index

Peggy, 71
RR, 60
T M, 60
T.M., 61
Thomas M, 65, 67, 68, 73
Thomas M., 60, 65, 72, 73
Thos. M., 68
TM, 60, 67
Hillard
  J., 89
  J.M., 90
  JM, Shff, 89
Hills
  Mr., 63
Holdhouser
  John, 66
Holland
  Baker, 71
  BE, 71
  G.F., 73
  John F, 76
  Thomas, 71
  Wm. J., 32
Holman
  D.W., 32
House
  Franklin, 35
  W.F., 31
  Wm. S., 38
Howard
  Dr., 154
  Dr. C.C., 149, 153, 155
  Dr. CC, 156
  Dr. J., 162
Howell
  William N., 55
Huggins
  Joel, 130, 131
  Joel A., 111
  Joel H., 120
Hughey
  George E., 52

Hull
  Franklin, 89
  Samuel B., 17
  W.D., 170
Hunter
  Lorenzo, 8, 17, 18
Hutchinson
  M., 13
  S N, 3
  S.N., 3
  Wm., 8, 17
Hyanes
  M.E., 59

I

Irwin
  A.R., 8
  Batte, 8, 17

J

J A Huggins & Co, 111
Jacobs
  Amos, 21, 22, 25, 42, 43
  Mr., 22
  Mr. Amos, 22
James
  Jos., 162
  Joseph, 160
  Lee S., 160
  Thomas A., 139, 147, 148
  Whitman, 153
Jennings
  SJ, 91
Johnson
  Amos, 22, 23
  Col. R.M., 151
  Marry Ann, 22

  Mary Ann, 21, 22, 23
  R J, 27
  R M, 29, 146, 151, 157
  R.F., 89
  R.M., 28, 29, 34, 40, 138, 146, 160
  Richard, 70, 143
  Richard M, 138, 153
  Richard M., 146, 147, 149
  RM, 28, 29, 139, 146, 158
  S., 89, 92, 106, 108
  Stephen, 86, 87, 88, 89, 90, 91, 92, 93, 94, 95, 106, 108
Johnson & Co., 147
Johnsons
  R., 70
Johnston
  Amos, 24
  R.F., 89, 91
  R.M., 31, 137, 147, 151
  Richard M, 148
  Richard M., 137
  RM, 147
  Robert F., 55
  S.T., 87
Jones
  Bill, a free boy, 44
  Mr., 35
  Nancy, 13
  W.B., 40
  William, 35
  Wm., 34

Index

K

keaton
  Silas, 162
Keaton
  S., 29
  Silas, 28, 29, 36, 39, 151, 159
Keatons
  Mr., 151
Kelley
  J A, 87
  J.A., 87
Kelly
  A., JP, 139
  Hugh, JP, 137
  J A, 89, 93, 95
  J.A., 89, 91, 92, 94
  JA, 87, 90, 91, 92, 106
  James, 175
  James A, 88, 89, 90, 93, 94, 99
  James A., 87, 88, 90, 92, 95, 96, 99, 102
  Jas A, 91
  Mr., 97
  Mr. James A., 97
  Sarah A., 90
Kenneday
  A.A., 13
Kerfeese
  C.S., 55
  Caleb S., 55
Kerr
  Andrew, 30, 31, 32, 33, 58
  Geo. S., 135
  George W., 31, 32
  J B, Clk, 6
  J.B., Clk, 9, 10, 12, 19

J.B., Coroner, 171
J.W.A., 66
JB, Clk, 4, 10, 11, 18, 19
JB, CSC, 10
Jennings B., Clk, 10, 19
  John, 71
  Mary, 80
  N.C., 65, 66, 67, 72
  NC, 68, 72
  Thos. L., 83
Kilpatrick
  A B, 36
  A.B., 38
  AB, 40
  Mrs., 43
Kirk
  John, 8
  John, Senr., 17

L

L.Q. Sharpes Law Office, 147
L.Q. Sharpes Law Office in the town of Statesville, 139
Lackie
  J W, 80
Lang
  Dr., 37, 38
Larance
  Dr., 61
Laughlin
  M., 37
Laurance
  Ingram, 76
Laurence
  Ingram, 74, 76
Lawrence
  A.A., 64, 72, 73
  Dr., 61, 72
  Dr. A., 70, 71
  Dr. A.A., 60
  Dr. AA, 64
  Ingram, 74
  Mr., 151
  Sarah, 70
Leckie
  J.H., 81
  J.H., DS, 81
  J.W., 80
  John, 80
  John W., 81
Lee
  Wm, 8, 18
  Wm., 8, 17
Lemly
  TB, 133
  Thomas, 125, 127
Leruly
  Jacob, 66
Lewis
  Jonathan, 8, 17, 18
Lewis
  Jonathan, 8
Linster
  RO, 159
Little
  S W, 56
  S.W., 56, 57
Litton
  Logan, 120, 121, 122, 129, 130, 132
Lockie
  John, 80
Logan
  A., 129
Long
  Dr. J.F., 40, 161
  J W, 125
  J.F., 159, 160
  J.W., 31, 125, 126
  John, 115, 116, 117, 128, 132

Index

John W, 113, 119, 124, 126, 127
John W., 113, 117, 118, 120, 123, 124, 132
JW, 109, 115, 127
Mr., 109, 110, 111, 112, 113, 118
W A, 120
W.A., 115
William H., 113
Wm H, 131
Wm. H, 131
Wm. H., 130
Lowry
  James M, 40
Luckey
  Robert, 50, 51
  Robt, 50
  Robt., 50
Lummis
  Charles, 82
Lunday
  B B, 34, 46
  B.B., 34
Lundy
  D B, 48
  B B, 36, 45, 49
  B B., 49
  B., 46
  B.B., 45, 46
  BB, 49

M

Manly
  M.E., Judge, 6
Marlow
  Mary, 27
  W.P, 30
  William P., 26
  Wm P, 26, 27, 29
  Wm. P, 26
  Wm. P., 27, 28
  WP, 29
Martin
  P.R., 55
  Pleasant R., 55
Maxwell
  F.H., 8, 17
  John G, 8, 17
  John G., 8, 17
Mc Grader
  Isaiah, 91
Mc Laughlin
  R.A., Clk, 45
  R.A., CSC, 42
  RA, Clk, 74
McClamroch
  James, 55
McCrae
  Dr., 154, 155
  Dr. C., 153, 156
McCulloh
  James, 55
McEwen
  Silas A., 31
McGradey
  Patrick K., 106
McGreedy
  Patrick, 92
McIntosh
  A.C., 13
Mclaughlin
  John H, 157
McLaughlin
  J.H., 158
  James, 38
  James H., 44, 71
  Jas H., DC, 64
  Jas. H., Jailor, 37
  JH, 157
  John H., 25, 31
  R A, 48
  R A, Clk, 40, 46
  R A, CSC, 54, 64
  R.A., Clk, 38, 39, 41, 46, 48, 49, 58, 70, 71, 75
  R.A., CSC, 37, 38, 51, 66, 89, 92, 93, 134, 135, 138, 148
  RA, Clerk, 75, 76
  RA, Clk, 44, 51, 83
  RA, CLK, 72
  RA, CSC, 47, 65, 66, 68, 72, 74, 82, 90, 93, 94, 134, 135, 146, 148, 149
McLauglin
  John H., 31
McLean
  John F., 32
Mclelland
  John, 147
McLelland
  Dr., 146
  J O, 137, 158, 170
  J.O., 137, 140, 147, 149, 158, 170
  Jno O, 157
  John, 149
  John O, 138, 157
  John O., 136, 137, 146, 147, 148, 150, 152, 153, 157, 158
  Mr., 151, 152
  WP, 13
McLellands
  John O., 151
McLocklin
  H., 36
McLoud
  Napoleon, 84
  R.L., 84
McNeely

Index

Robert, 8
Robert A, 18
Robert A., 8, 17
W.K., 171
McNeil
  J.W.S., JP, 108
  JWS, JP, 106
  Wm., JP, 93
McNeily
  Ebenezer, 170
Meade
  Jos., 13
Means
  Charles T., 17
  Chs. T, 8
  Wm, 17
  Wm., 8, 17
Meanse
  Wm., 8
Meroney
  M.A., Shff, 91
  Mr. A., Shff, 108
  Mr., Shff, 108
  Philip F., 55
  W.A., Sheriff, 57
  William A.,
    Sheriff, 55, 56
  Wm A, Shff, 53
  Wm. A., Shff, 52
Miller
  Mathias, 55
  William M., 8
  Wilson N., 17
Milligan
  James, 71
  M.W., 31
Mills
  George, 135
  R.L., 32
  R.S., 31
Millsaps
  Hezekiah, 70
Mitchel
  A., Judge, 156
Mitchell

A., 132
A., Judge, 166
Monson
Mr. E., 170
Montgomery
  J.E., Coroner, 170
Moose
  W.A., Shff, 53
Morgan
  B, 166
  B., 166
  Bart., 166
  Bartlet, 166, 167
Morgan District
  Court, 20
Morrison
  A.R., 31
Mr Keatons Bottom,
  151
Mundy
  Benjamin, 32
Murdoch
  James, 69
Murdock
  James, 70
  James:, 71
Myers
  Wm., Foreman,
    31

N

Nash
  Benj. H., 96, 105
  Benjamin H.,
    Attorney, 95
NC Counties
  Caldwell, 90
  Davie, 52, 53, 55,
    56, 57, 87, 88,
    89, 91, 95
  Mecklenburg, 3,
    5, 6, 7, 9, 10,

    11, 14, 16, 17,
    18, 20
  Wilkes, 86, 90,
    91, 92, 93, 95,
    106, 108
NC Towns
  Charlotte, 6, 8,
    12, 17, 130
  Mocksville, 55,
    57, 94, 106
Neill
  T., 171
Nesbet
  M.L., 133
Nesbit
  M L, 134
  M.T., 159
  ML, 134
Nicholson
  Thomas, 54
  Thos., 54
Nixon
  Dr., 99, 105
  Dr. Thomas M.,
    87
Nixson
  Dr., 88
  Thos., Physician,
    88
Normant
  W.S., 13

O

Oates
  B., Clk, 17
Oatsman
  John, 26
Hatcher & McGee,
  94
Ormand
  Robert, 8, 17
Owens
  Franklin, 91

Index

P

Parker
  B.W., 55
  Dr., 88, 94, 99
  Dr. Wm W, 105
  Dr. Wm. W., 87, 88, 102
  Jacob, 109, 110, 117, 125, 126, 133, 159
  Wm W, M.D., 88, 105
  Wm. W., 87, 95
  Wm. W., M.D., 88
Parkes
  Jacob, 133, 134
Parks
  D.C., 85
  R H, 85
  R.H., 84
  RH, Junr., 84
  Richard D, 86
  Richard H, 85
  Richard H., 84, 85, 86
Peebles
  Nathaniel A., 55
Penry
  Thomas S., 55
Perry
  Calvin, 170
Philips
  W.G., 8, 17
Pleasant
  James, Commissioner, 88
Pleasants
  James, 88
  James, Commissioner, 95, 98, 102, 105
Plummer
  George, 4
Pollard
  Dr., 99
  Th., M.D., 88
Poston
  Hiel L., 31
  John E., 32

R

R M Johnson & Co., 157
R.M. Johnson & Co, 137, 141, 153
R.M. Johnson & Co., 136, 158
R.M. Johnson &C, 137
R.M. Johnston & Co, 147, 148, 149
R.M. Johnston & Co., 146
McLaughlin, 92
Radiner
  Thos, 27
Ramseur
  Jacob, 134
Ramsour
  Jacob, 133, 134
Rea
  William, Foreman, 18
  Wm, 8
  Wm., 8, 17
  Wm., Foreman, 9
Rector
  Silas, 40, 160
Redman
  A., 160, 162
  Alexander, 163
  John, 163

T.W., 28, 29
Thos, 28, 29
Thos., 28
Thos. W., 28
Regulations Concerning Slaves, 169
Reid
  Mrs. J.M., 170
  R.S., 13
  Robert S, 15
Reynolds
  H., 143
  Hugh, 80, 137, 138, 147, 148, 149, 153, 157, 158, 174
  Mr., 138, 152
  Mr. Hugh, 147, 151
Rhyne
  Joseph N, 18
  Joseph N., 8, 17
Richard M Johnson & Co, 157
Rickert
  SJ, 159
Rivers
  South, 142, 151
  Yadkin, 139
Robb
  Thomas J., 23
  Thos. J., 21
Robey
  A., 174
  Absalom, 174
Robinson
  James B., 17
  Jas B., 8
  Jas. B, 8
  Jas. B., 17
Robison
  H.E., 31
Ross
  F M, 2

193

Index

F.M., 1, 2, 13
F.M., JP, 3
FM, 2
Francis W., 5
James N, 17
James N., 17
Jas. N, 8
Jas. N., 8
Royden
 N., Sol., 123
Rumple
 David, 159
 Dick, 159
 Joseph L., 171

S

Sanders
 F., 34
 F.M., 36
 William,
  Solicitor, 10
 Wm., Solicitor, 19
Saunders
 Francis M., 40
SC Towns
 Sumpterville, 84
Scroggs
 A.A., 90
 Dr. AA, 90
 Ephraim, 30
 J.H., JP, 67
Bobbit, 164
Sharp & Sharpe, 120
Sharpe
 A P, 157
 A.P., 158
 A.P., JP, 164
 Alfred, 77
 AP, 157, 159
 David, 143
 Silas D., JP, 21
Sharpe & Sharpe,
 130

Shaw
 R., 13
 R.R., 13
Sheek
 Daniel S., 55
Shepherd
 James, 171
Simonton
 A K, 157
 A.K., 138, 143,
  147, 158, 162
 J.R., 174
 J.R.,
  Commissioner,
  174
 Johnson, 170
 JR, 175
 K.T., JP, 59
 R.F., 157, 158
 R.F., JP, 59
 RF, JP, 59
 Ross, 146
Slaves
 Amos, 61, 63
 Ben, 96, 97, 99,
  100, 106, 107
 Ben Franklin, 88,
  102
 Benjamin
  Franklin, 96
 Buck, 52, 53, 54,
  56, 57
 Casse, 119, 120,
  121, 122
 Cassey, 113, 115
 Cassie, 120, 130,
  131
 Cassy, 109, 110,
  114, 115, 130
 Cassy, a
  licentious
  woman., 109
 Cynthia, 174
 Delia, 171

Delia, Inquest of.,
 170
Demps, 85, 86
Dick, 60, 62, 64,
 65, 66, 67, 68,
 69, 72, 138,
 139, 140, 141,
 142, 143, 144,
 145, 150, 151,
 152, 153, 154,
 155, 156, 157,
 170
Dicks, 144, 151,
 152
Easter, 73, 74, 76
Edmund, 35, 40
Elias, 63, 71
Elon, 174
Frank, 52, 53, 54,
 56, 57
Frederick, 175
George, 50, 51
Hiram, 49
Hugh, 52, 53, 54,
 56, 57
Ike, 69, 70, 71,
 72, 73
Isaac, 35, 60, 61,
 62, 63, 64, 66
Isabella, 163
Jack, 162, 163
Jesse, 174
Jim, 109, 110,
 111, 115, 116,
 117, 118, 119,
 120, 121, 122,
 123, 126, 128,
 129, 130, 131,
 132
Les, 35
Louisa, 61, 64, 70
Mary, 44
Melmoth, 170
Melmoth, Inquest
 of., 170

Index

Metmoth, 170
Mimi, 174
Mina, 163
Minda, 161
Nelson, 31
Preedy, 175
Rufus, 21, 22, 23,
  24, 25
Sandy, 59
Silva Jones, a
  Slave, 13
Thornton, 29, 30
Thornton, a
  runaway, 30
Thorton, 28
Tom, 1, 2, 3, 4, 5,
  6, 7, 8, 9, 10,
  11, 12, 14, 15,
  16, 18, 19, 20
Will, 85, 86
Wilson, 34, 35,
  37, 38, 39, 40,
  41, 42
Wilsons, 37
Worrey, 13
Smith
  H., 84
  Hiram, 84, 85, 86
  Mr. Hiram, 84
  Samuel, 55
Somers
  Charles S., JP,
    148
South Carolina
  Sumter Hotel, 84
Speck
  John, 80
Staly
  E, Shff, 94, 95
  E., Shff, 84, 86,
    92, 94
  Esly, Sheriff, 85
States
  Alabama, 61, 134,
    140, 146, 147,

149, 153, 155,
  156, 160, 161,
  162
  Georgia, 160
  South Carolina, 5,
    84
  Virginia, 87, 88,
    95
Stayley
  E, 27
Stimpson
  E.B., 170
Stimson
  E B, Clk, 82
  E.B., Clerk, 80
  E.B., Clk, 81
  EB, Clerk, 80
  EB, Clk, 80, 81,
    82
Stinson
  Mr., 71
  William, 8
  Wm., 17
Stone
  Elijah, 159
  Eliza, 142
  R.A., 141, 148,
    159
  R.F., 159
  W F, 27, 142
  W.F., 148
  WF, 29
  Wm. F., 26, 141,
    147
Summer
  CS, Shff, 81
  Mr., 43
Summers
  C.L., Clerk, 5
  C.L., Clk, 3, 83,
    85, 165
  C.L., CSC, 158
  C.S., Clk, 4, 5, 7,
    14, 15, 16, 23,
    24, 26, 27, 30,

33, 157, 158,
  167
C.S., JP, 153
CL, Clk, 4
CL, Shff, 80
CS, 70
CS, Clerk, 24
CS, Clk, 8, 26, 29,
  69, 77
CS, CSC, 166
Frank, 70
Hiram, 24
J.E., JP, 34
James, JP, 42
Thomas, 21, 22,
  23, 25
Thos., 21, 22, 24
W., 44

T

Tatum
  Ezra W., 55
  S.O., 55
  Samuel O., 55
Taylor
  Jenkins, 130
  MB, 13
Templeman
  H.N., 87, 94
  Mr. H.N., 96
Templeton
  Ephraim, 32
  John, Foreman,
    40
  R.R., 171
  Thos, 170
Terry
  John, 115
Thorn
  D.C., 171
Thornton
  James C., 55
Tomlin

Index

N.D., Forman, 51
P, JP, 164
P., JP, 164
Tomlinson
  H., 170
  Thomas W., 32
Torrence
  H.M., 49
  One, 13
  Oni, 5, 13
  P., 5
Trautman
  H., Shff, 25
Trinity Church, 63
Trollenger
  Jacob, 133
Troutman
  A., 31, 32, 129
  Absalom, 120
  H, Shff, 15, 23, 26
  H., Shff, 3, 15, 23, 24, 30, 83, 84
Tucker
  James, 32
  James A., 175
  Nancy, 176
  T.S., 163, 164, 165
  TS, 165
Turner
  J.M., 175, 176
  J.M., Commissioner, 175
  JM, 175
  W., Foreman, 46
Tuttle
  RG, Shff, 90

V

VA Towns

Richmond, 87, 95, 97, 98, 102
Vanderburg
  Levi, 31, 32
Virginia Towns
  Richmond, 94

W

Caldwell, 110
Walker
  Alonzo, 13
Wallace
  E.C., 8, 17
  EC, 17
  James, Senr., 17
  Jas, 8
Warren
  W., Shff, 147
wasson
  DA, 147
Wasson
  D., 170
  D.A., 147, 149, 158, 170
  DA, 157
  David, 136, 137, 138, 146, 147, 148, 149, 153
  David A, 148, 150
  David A., 137
  JA, 137
  Mr., 152
  W F, Shff, 125, 126
  W.F., 23, 24, 25, 54
  W.F., DS, 84
  W.F., Shff, 37, 38, 39, 41, 49, 58, 60, 66, 70, 71, 73, 127, 135, 136, 137, 146, 158, 167

WF, 66
WF, DS, 23
WF, Shff, 69, 71, 75, 124, 125, 137
Watts
  D.S., 48
  George, 61, 63
  James A., 31
  R, Shff, 13
  T.W., DS, 126
  Thos, 170
  W T, DS, 125
  W.S., 49
  W.S., DS, 50
  W.T., DS, 58, 125, 135
  Wm. H., 63
  WT, DS, 124
  Z.W.T., DS, 127
Webber
  Adam, 36
Weber
  A., 35
Welch
  Jos, 45
  Joseph, 46, 47
Welsh
  Jos, 48
  Jos., 45
  Joseph, 48
West
  Jo. S., 118
  Joseph, 113
Westmoreland
  W.L., 31
White
  J.N., 66
  J.W., 67
  James Junr., 55
  John, 65, 70
  M.A., 66
  R.W., 5
  Robert, 5, 6, 7
Whitman

Index

James K.,
  Commissioner, 149
James, Storehouse
  of., 156
Jas K., 156
Whittington
  Alexander, 92
  Alexr., 92
  Allen, 92
  Elizabeth, 92
  Sarah, 90, 106, 108
Wilcoxson
  Wm., 91
Williams
  J.W., 162, 170
Willson

R.L., Constable, 21
Wilson
  D., 27
  R.L., Constable, 25
Witherspoon
  Wm. H., DShff, 93
  Parker, 102
Wolf
  Tobias, 8, 17
Woodward
  Dempsey, 31
Wool Cording Machine, 62
Wooly
  C.A., 75

Wren
  M.A., 44
Wright
  John W., DS, 88
Wyatt
  George, 91, 106

Young
  John, 13, 111, 112, 117, 123, 126, 133, 135
  Robert H., 8, 17

ABOUT THE AUTHORS

WILLIAM L. BYRD, III has been involved in genealogical and historical research for more than thirty years. His primary areas of interest are Native Americans, African Americans, West Indians, East Indians and Moors in Virginia, North Carolina, and South Carolina. He has been published by the *North Carolina Genealogical Society Journal*, the *Magazine of Virginia Genealogy*, *The Rowan County Register*, and *The South Carolina Magazine of Ancestral Research*. He has also co-authored articles with Sheila Stover in the *North Carolina Genealogical Society Journal*, *The Augustan Society Omnibus*, the *Pan-American Indian Association News*, and the *Eagle: New England's American Indian Journal*. He has received an "Award of Special Recognition" from The North Carolina Society of Historians in the category of "The History Article Award" for preserving North Carolina history.

He is a U.S. Army Veteran from the Vietnam era, and served with the U.S. Armed Forces overseas. He is currently retired, and resides with his family in Hickory, North Carolina.

ೞ ೕ

JOHN H. SMITH holds a BA in psychology from Lenoir Rhyne College, and did his graduate work at Winthrop University. His professional memberships include American Psychological Association, and Phi Alpha Theta (National Honor Society in History.) In addition to his full-time career, Mr. Smith is a part-time continuing education instructor of genealogy and family history, and a part-time research assistant to Catawba County Historical Association.

Mr. Smith was the editor of *The Burke Journal* (1992-1995), a quarterly publication of the Burke County Genealogical Society, (winner of the *Excellence in Periodical Publishing Award* from the North Carolina Genealogical Society, 1995.) He has presented numerous programs to genealogical groups in North Carolina in the past fifteen years, and has twice been a speaker at the South Carolina Genealogical Society's summer workshop. His articles have been published in *The Burke Journal*, *Catawba Cousins*, the *Rowan Register*, the *South Carolina Magazine of Ancestral Research* and several other local/county quarterlies.

Other Heritage Books by William L. Byrd, III:

Against the Peace and Dignity of the State: North Carolina Laws Regarding Slaves, Free Persons of Color, and Indians

Bladen County, North Carolina Tax Lists: 1768 through 1774, Volume I

Bladen County, North Carolina Tax Lists: 1775 through 1789, Volume II

For So Long as the Sun and Moon Endure: Indian Records from the North Carolina General Assembly Sessions, & Other Sources

In Full Force and Virtue: North Carolina Emancipation Records, 1713-1860

North Carolina General Assembly Sessions Records: Slaves and Free Persons of Color, 1709-1789

North Carolina Slaves and Free Persons of Color: Chowan County, Volume One

North Carolina Slaves and Free Persons of Color: Chowan County, Volume Two

North Carolina Slaves and Free Persons of Color: Pasquotank County

North Carolina Slaves and Free Persons of Color: Perquimans County

Villainy Often Goes Unpunished: Indian Records from the North Carolina General Assembly Sessions, 1675-1789

Other Heritage Books by William L. Byrd, III and John H. Smith:

North Carolina Slaves and Free Persons of Color: Burke, Lincoln, and Rowan Counties

North Carolina Slaves and Free Persons of Color: Hyde and Beaufort Counties

North Carolina Slaves and Free Persons of Color: Iredell County

North Carolina Slaves and Free Persons of Color: Mecklenburg, Gaston, and Union Counties

North Carolina Slaves and Free Persons of Color: McDowell County

North Carolina Slaves and Free Persons of Color: Stokes and Yadkin Counties

www.ingramcontent.com/pod-product-compliance
Lightning Source LLC
Chambersburg PA
CBHW050148170426
43197CB00011B/2006